First World War
and Army of Occupation
War Diary
France, Belgium and Germany

50 DIVISION
Divisional Troops
Divisional Trench Mortar Batteries
19 June 1915 - 31 January 1919

WO95/2820/2

The Naval & Military Press Ltd
www.nmarchive.com
Published in association with The National Archives

Published by

The Naval & Military Press Ltd

Unit 10 Ridgewood Industrial Park,

Uckfield, East Sussex,

TN22 5QE England

Tel: +44 (0) 1825 749494

www.naval-military-press.com

www.nmarchive.com

This diary has been reprinted in facsimile from the original. Any imperfections are inevitably reproduced and the quality may fall short of modern type and cartographic standards.

Contents

Document type	Place/Title	Date From	Date To
Heading	WO95/2820 50 Div. Div. Trench Mortar Batteries Aug' 15-Jan 19.		
Heading	50th Division Trench Mortar Batts. 1915 Aug-Jan 1919		
Heading	X 50 Trench Mortar Late 31. Bty Vol III		
War Diary		16/08/1915	22/08/1915
War Diary	Armentieres	23/08/1915	26/09/1915
War Diary	In The Field C 25 C 1.7	01/11/1915	10/11/1915
War Diary	Sheet 27 W 19 D 38	11/11/1915	15/11/1915
War Diary	In The Field Sheet 27 W 19 D 38	16/11/1915	30/11/1915
War Diary	Sheet 27 W 19 a 38	01/12/1915	19/12/1915
War Diary	Still 60 Sheet 28 N.W. Z.29 680	19/12/1915	19/12/1915
Heading	31st Trench Mortar Bty Jan Vol VII		
War Diary	Sheet 28 I 29 C 1.4	10/01/1916	31/01/1916
Heading	31 Trench Mortar Bty Feb Vol II		
War Diary	I 29.c.1.5. Sheet 28	01/02/1916	29/02/1916
War Diary	I.29.c.3.2.	01/03/1916	01/03/1916
War Diary	I.29.c.3.4. 1/2	01/03/1916	01/03/1916
War Diary	I.29.c.4.5	02/03/1916	02/03/1916
War Diary	I.29.c.3.2	02/03/1916	02/03/1916
War Diary	I.29.c. 4 3/4 1 1/2	02/03/1916	02/03/1916
War Diary	I.29.c.5.1 1/2	02/03/1916	02/03/1916
War Diary	I.29.c 4 1/3.1	02/03/1916	03/03/1916
War Diary	I.29.c.4.5	04/03/1916	09/03/1916
War Diary	I.29.c. 1.4. 1/2	09/03/1916	09/03/1916
War Diary	I.29.c.4.2	09/03/1916	09/03/1916
War Diary	I.29.c.4.5	10/03/1916	10/03/1916
War Diary	I.29.c.4.2	10/03/1916	10/03/1916
War Diary	I.29.c.4.5	11/03/1916	11/03/1916
War Diary	I.29.c.1.4 1/2	11/03/1916	11/03/1916
War Diary	I.29.c.1.4 1/2	12/03/1916	13/03/1916
War Diary	I.29.c.6.3.	13/03/1916	13/03/1916
War Diary	I.29.c.4.5	13/03/1916	13/03/1916
War Diary	I.29.c.1. 4 1/2	14/03/1916	15/03/1916
War Diary	I.29.c.1. 4 1/3	15/03/1916	17/03/1916
War Diary	I.29.c.1.4 1/2	17/03/1916	21/03/1916
War Diary	I.29.c.4.5	21/03/1916	21/03/1916
War Diary	I.29.c.1.4 1/2	22/03/1916	22/03/1916
War Diary	I.29.c.3.2	22/03/1916	22/03/1916
War Diary	The Bluff (Ypres-Comines Canal)	23/03/1916	31/03/1916
War Diary	The Bluff	31/03/1916	31/03/1916
Heading	X 50 TM Bty Vol IV		
War Diary	I.29.c.4.5.	01/04/1916	01/04/1916
War Diary	I.29.d. 6 1/2.0	02/04/1916	05/04/1916
War Diary	N.28.c.8.7	05/04/1916	06/04/1916
War Diary	I.24.c.3 1/2. 7 1/2	06/04/1916	06/04/1916
War Diary	N.18.c.8.7	06/04/1916	06/04/1916
War Diary		07/04/1916	07/04/1916
War Diary	I.29.a.2.0	08/04/1916	08/04/1916
War Diary	I.29.b.1.5	08/04/1916	09/04/1916
War Diary	N29.c 1/2 9	10/04/1916	10/04/1916

War Diary	N 29.d 2.9	10/04/1916	10/04/1916
War Diary	N29.d 3.8	10/04/1916	10/04/1916
War Diary	N29.d 2.9	11/04/1916	11/04/1916
War Diary	N29.c 3.8	12/04/1916	12/04/1916
War Diary	N 30.c. 3.0	13/04/1916	14/04/1916
War Diary	N 30.d. 0.7	14/04/1916	14/04/1916
War Diary	N 30.d.2.9	14/04/1916	16/04/1916
War Diary	N 29.c 1/2 9	17/04/1916	17/04/1916
War Diary	N 30.b.2.0	17/04/1916	17/04/1916
War Diary	N 30.c.2.0	18/04/1916	18/04/1916
War Diary	N 30.c.1.5	18/04/1916	18/04/1916
War Diary	N 30.c.2.0	18/04/1916	18/04/1916
War Diary	N 29.b.2.0	18/04/1916	18/04/1916
War Diary	N 24.c.1.5	18/04/1916	19/04/1916
War Diary	N 29.6.2.0	19/04/1916	19/04/1916
War Diary	N 24.c.1.5	19/04/1916	19/04/1916
War Diary	N 30.c.2.0	19/04/1916	19/04/1916
War Diary	N 29.b.2.0	19/04/1916	19/04/1916
War Diary	N 29.c.3.3	19/04/1916	19/04/1916
War Diary	N 24.c.1.5	19/04/1916	19/04/1916
War Diary	N 29.c.3.3	20/04/1916	20/04/1916
War Diary	N 24.c.1.5.	20/04/1916	20/04/1916
War Diary	N 29.b.2.0	20/04/1916	20/04/1916
War Diary	N 24.c.1.5	20/04/1916	22/04/1916
War Diary	N 29.b.2.0	23/04/1916	23/04/1916
War Diary	N 29.c. 1/2.9	23/04/1916	23/04/1916
War Diary	N 24 C.2.5.	23/04/1916	23/04/1916
War Diary	N 30 C.3.0	23/04/1916	24/04/1916
War Diary	N 29 C.3.8	25/04/1916	25/04/1916
War Diary	N 30 C 3.0	26/04/1916	26/04/1916
War Diary	N 24 C 2.5	27/04/1916	27/04/1916
War Diary	N 30 C 3.0	28/04/1916	28/04/1916
War Diary	N 30 C 5.2	29/04/1916	29/04/1916
War Diary	N 29.c.2.9	30/04/1916	02/05/1916
War Diary	Q.28.d 1.7	03/05/1916	26/05/1916
War Diary	N 29.c.4.3.	26/05/1916	28/05/1916
War Diary	N 30.c.2.0	28/05/1916	28/05/1916
War Diary	N 24.c.1.5	28/05/1916	28/05/1916
War Diary	N 30.c.2.0	28/05/1916	28/05/1916
War Diary	N 29.b.2.0	28/05/1916	28/05/1916
War Diary	N 24.c.1.5	28/05/1916	28/05/1916
War Diary	N 29.a.8.2	28/05/1916	28/05/1916
War Diary	N 29.c.4.3	28/05/1916	28/05/1916
War Diary	N 29.b.7 1/2. 1 1/2	29/05/1916	29/05/1916
War Diary	N 24.c.1.5	29/05/1916	29/05/1916
War Diary	N 30.c.2.0	29/05/1916	29/05/1916
War Diary	N 29.d.7 1/2 3 1/2	29/05/1916	29/05/1916
War Diary	N 29.b. 7 1/2 3 1/2	29/05/1916	29/05/1916
War Diary	N 29.d. 7 1/2 3 1/2	30/05/1916	30/05/1916
War Diary	N 29.b.7 1/2 3 1/2	30/05/1916	30/05/1916
War Diary	N 29.c.4.3	30/05/1916	30/05/1916
War Diary	N 29.b.7 1/3. 1 1/2	31/05/1916	31/05/1916
War Diary	N 29.d.7 1/3. 1 1/2	31/05/1916	31/05/1916
War Diary	N 29.b.2.0. N.30.b.2.0	31/05/1916	31/05/1916
War Diary	N 29.b. 7 1/2 1 1/2. N 29.d. 7 1/2. 3 1/2.	01/06/1916	01/06/1916
War Diary	N 29.d. 7 1/2. 3 1/2. N 29.b. 7 1/2. 3 1/2.	02/06/1916	02/06/1916

War Diary	N 29.b. 2.0	02/06/1916	02/06/1916
War Diary	N 30.c.2.0	02/06/1916	02/06/1916
War Diary	N 30.b.2.0	02/06/1916	02/06/1916
War Diary	N 24.c.1.5	02/06/1916	02/06/1916
War Diary	N 29.b. 7 1/2, 1 1/2	02/06/1916	02/06/1916
War Diary	N 29.d. 7 1/2. 3 1/2.	03/06/1916	03/06/1916
War Diary	N 30.c.2.0	03/06/1916	03/06/1916
War Diary	N.29.d. 7 1/2, 3 1/2	03/06/1916	03/06/1916
War Diary	N.29.b.2.0	04/06/1916	04/06/1916
War Diary	N.30.c.2.0	04/06/1916	04/06/1916
War Diary	N.24.c.1.5	04/06/1916	04/06/1916
War Diary	N.29.c. 4.3	04/06/1916	04/06/1916
War Diary	N.29.d. 7 1/3, 3 1/2	05/06/1916	05/06/1916
War Diary	N.30.c.2.0	05/06/1916	05/06/1916
War Diary	N.29.c.4.3	05/06/1916	05/06/1916
War Diary	N.29.b.2.0	06/06/1916	06/06/1916
War Diary	N.29.d. 7 1/2. 3 1/2	06/06/1916	06/06/1916
War Diary	N.29.c.6.6	06/06/1916	06/06/1916
War Diary	N.24.c.1.5	06/06/1916	06/06/1916
War Diary	N.29.d 7 1/2 3 1/2	07/06/1916	08/06/1916
War Diary	N. 29.b. 2.0	08/06/1916	08/06/1916
War Diary	N.30.c.2.0	08/06/1916	08/06/1916
War Diary	N.29.d 7 1/2. 3 1/2.	09/06/1916	09/06/1916
War Diary	N.29.b.2.0	09/06/1916	09/06/1916
War Diary	N.30.b. 2 1/2.0	09/06/1916	10/06/1916
War Diary	N.30.c.2.0	10/06/1916	10/06/1916
War Diary	N.29.d. 7 1/2. 3 1/2	10/06/1916	11/06/1916
War Diary	N.29.b.20.	11/06/1916	12/06/1916
War Diary	N.29.d.7.7	13/06/1916	13/06/1916
War Diary	N.24.c.1.5.	14/06/1916	14/06/1916
War Diary	N.29.d. 7 1/2. 3 1/2	14/06/1916	14/06/1916
War Diary	N.30.c.2.0.	14/06/1916	14/06/1916
War Diary	N.30.a.2.0	14/06/1916	14/06/1916
War Diary	N.30.a.1.6 1/2	15/06/1916	15/06/1916
War Diary	N.29.d. 7 1/2. 3 1/2.	15/06/1916	15/06/1916
War Diary	N.24.c.1.5.	16/06/1916	16/06/1916
War Diary	N.29.6.2.0	16/06/1916	16/06/1916
War Diary	N.30.a.1. 6 1/2	16/06/1916	16/06/1916
War Diary	N.24.c.1.5.	16/06/1916	16/06/1916
War Diary	N.29.b.2.0	16/06/1916	16/06/1916
War Diary	N.29.d. 7 1/2. 3 1/2	16/06/1916	16/06/1916
War Diary	N.29.d. 7 1/2. 3 1/2.	17/06/1916	17/06/1916
War Diary	N.24.c.1.5.	17/06/1916	17/06/1916
War Diary	N.30.b.2.0	17/06/1916	17/06/1916
War Diary	N.30.a.1.6 1/2	17/06/1916	17/06/1916
War Diary	N.29.b.2.0	17/06/1916	17/06/1916
War Diary	N.29.c.8.6	17/06/1916	17/06/1916
War Diary	N.30.a.1.6 1/2	17/06/1916	17/06/1916
War Diary	N.24.c.1.5	17/06/1916	17/06/1916
War Diary	N.30.a 1.6 1/2	18/06/1916	18/06/1916
War Diary	N.29.b.2.0	18/06/1916	18/06/1916
War Diary	N.30.a 1.6 1/2	19/06/1916	20/06/1916
War Diary	N.24.c.1.5	21/06/1916	21/06/1916
War Diary	N.29.d 7 1/2 3 1/2	21/06/1916	21/06/1916
War Diary	N.24.c.1.5	22/06/1916	22/06/1916
War Diary	N.29.d. 7 1/2. 3 1/2	22/06/1916	22/06/1916

War Diary	N.29.c.6.6	22/06/1916	22/06/1916
War Diary	N.29.d 7 1/2. 3 1/2	22/06/1916	22/06/1916
War Diary	N.29.c 7 1/2. 3 1/2	23/06/1916	23/06/1916
War Diary	N.28.b.b.9	24/06/1916	24/06/1916
War Diary	N.29.c.6.6	25/06/1916	25/06/1916
War Diary	N.29.d. 7 1/2. 3 1/2	26/06/1916	26/06/1916
War Diary	N.29.b.2.0	26/06/1916	26/06/1916
War Diary	N.29.d. 7 1/2. 3 1/2	26/06/1916	27/06/1916
War Diary	N.30.a.1.6 1/2	27/06/1916	27/06/1916
War Diary	N.29.b.2.0	27/06/1916	27/06/1916
War Diary	N.24.c.1.5	27/06/1916	27/06/1916
War Diary	N.29.d. 7 1/2. 3 1/2	28/06/1916	28/06/1916
War Diary	N. 24.c.1.5	28/06/1916	28/06/1916
War Diary	N.29.b.2.0	29/06/1916	29/06/1916
War Diary	N.29.d. 7 1/2. 3 1/2	29/06/1916	29/06/1916
War Diary	N.30.a.1.6 1/2.	29/06/1916	29/06/1916
War Diary	N.24.c.1.5.	29/06/1916	30/06/1916
War Diary	N.29.b.2.0	30/06/1916	30/06/1916
War Diary	N.29.d. 7 1/2 3 1/2.	30/06/1916	30/06/1916
War Diary	Bois Berques	13/08/1916	13/08/1916
War Diary	Sheet 62 D. B.18.a.8.1	14/08/1916	27/08/1916
War Diary	Sheet 57 D. W 26 C 3.4	28/08/1916	31/08/1916
Heading	50th. Divisional Artillery 50th. Div. Trench Mortar Brigade September 1916		
War Diary	Sheet 57 D. W 26 C 34	01/09/1916	15/09/1916
War Diary	Sheet 57 D W.26b.3.0	16/09/1916	27/09/1916
War Diary	Sheet 57 C S.19.d 5.0	28/09/1916	30/09/1916
War Diary	Sheet 57 C S.19.d.6.2	01/10/1916	30/11/1916
War Diary	Sheet 62 D C.13.c.3.7	01/12/1916	13/12/1916
War Diary	B.12.c.4.8. Sheet 62.d.	14/12/1916	14/12/1916
War Diary	Sheet 62 D. B.12.c.4.8	15/12/1916	29/12/1916
War Diary	Sheet 57 D. S.19.a.5.0	30/12/1916	31/12/1916
War Diary	Sheet 57 D S.19.d.50.	01/01/1917	29/01/1917
War Diary	B.7.b.3.5	30/01/1917	05/02/1917
War Diary	Hamelet	06/02/1917	13/02/1917
War Diary	M.27.a.7.5	14/02/1917	14/02/1917
War Diary	Sheet 62c S.W M.2.d.75.	15/02/1917	28/02/1917
Miscellaneous	Headquarters, 50th Division.	02/04/1917	02/04/1917
War Diary	Sheet 62c S.W. M.27.d.7.5	01/03/1917	13/03/1917
War Diary	M.27.d.7.5	14/03/1917	22/03/1917
War Diary	Hamelet	23/03/1917	27/03/1917
War Diary	Occoches	28/03/1917	04/04/1917
War Diary	Wailly	05/04/1917	16/04/1917
War Diary	Arras.	17/04/1917	24/05/1917
War Diary	Monchiet	25/05/1917	17/06/1917
War Diary	Boiry Becquerelle	18/06/1917	02/09/1917
War Diary	T.7.a 6.4	03/09/1917	07/09/1917
War Diary	Boiry Becquerelle	07/09/1917	01/10/1917
War Diary	T.7.a.6.4	02/10/1917	08/10/1917
War Diary	Boiry Becquerelle. T.7.a.6.4	09/10/1917	21/10/1917
War Diary	T.7.a.6.4	22/10/1917	23/10/1917
War Diary	Sheet 28 Woeston	23/10/1917	25/10/1917
War Diary	B.10.d.8.4	26/10/1917	26/10/1917
War Diary	B.15.a.2.7	27/10/1917	30/11/1917
Heading	Y 50 T M Bty Vol 4		
War Diary	I.24 B. 5.5	31/01/1916	29/02/1916

War Diary	I 29.c.4.4. N 24.a.4.8	05/04/1916	30/04/1916
War Diary	Q.28.d.1.7	01/05/1916	31/05/1916
War Diary	N2	01/06/1916	02/06/1916
War Diary	O 7a 1 1/2, O 7a 75	03/06/1916	03/06/1916
War Diary	Old 4 1/2 2	04/06/1916	04/06/1916
War Diary	N 6 C 81	05/06/1916	06/06/1916
War Diary	O 7a 75	07/06/1916	07/06/1916
War Diary	O 7a 65	08/06/1916	08/06/1916
War Diary	O 7a 1 1/2	09/06/1916	09/06/1916
War Diary	O 7a 75	10/06/1916	10/06/1916
War Diary	N12 D 98	11/06/1916	11/06/1916
War Diary	O 7a 75	12/06/1916	12/06/1916
War Diary	Old 42	13/06/1916	14/06/1916
War Diary	N12d 98	14/06/1916	14/06/1916
War Diary	Old 42	15/06/1916	16/06/1916
War Diary	O 7a 1 1/2 1	16/06/1916	17/06/1916
War Diary	N12 D 98	18/06/1916	18/06/1916
War Diary	Old 42	19/06/1916	20/06/1916
War Diary	O 7a 75	20/06/1916	20/06/1916
War Diary	Old 42	21/06/1916	21/06/1916
War Diary	O 7a 1/2 1	21/06/1916	21/06/1916
War Diary	O 7a 75	22/06/1916	22/06/1916
War Diary	O 7a 1 1/2	22/06/1916	22/06/1916
War Diary	Old 4 1/2 2	23/06/1916	23/06/1916
War Diary	N 6a 22	23/06/1916	23/06/1916
War Diary	N12d 98	24/06/1916	24/06/1916
War Diary	O 7a 75	24/06/1916	24/06/1916
War Diary	Old 4 1/2 2	24/06/1916	24/06/1916
War Diary	O 7a 75	25/06/1916	25/06/1916
War Diary	N12d 98	25/06/1916	26/06/1916
War Diary	O 7a 75	26/06/1916	26/06/1916
War Diary	Old 4 1/2 2	26/06/1916	26/06/1916
War Diary	O 7a 75	26/06/1916	26/06/1916
War Diary	N12d 98	27/06/1916	27/06/1916
War Diary	Old 4 1/2 2	28/06/1916	28/06/1916
War Diary	N 12 D 8.1	29/06/1916	29/06/1916
War Diary	N12 D 98	30/06/1916	30/06/1916
War Diary	O 7a 1 1/2 1	30/06/1916	30/06/1916
War Diary	O 7a 75	30/06/1916	30/06/1916
War Diary	O 7a 1 1/2 1	30/06/1916	30/06/1916
War Diary	In The Field	30/11/1915	02/12/1915
War Diary	Belgium	19/12/1915	27/12/1915
War Diary	Sheet 28 I.24.d.5.5	10/01/1916	16/01/1916
War Diary	Lanctuary Wood	16/01/1916	24/01/1916
War Diary	I.24 D.55 Sheet 28	24/01/1916	31/01/1916
Heading	29 Trench Motar Bty Jan Vol I From Jan 1915		
War Diary	In The Field	19/06/1915	24/06/1915
Miscellaneous	Instruction to O.C. 29th. Trench Howitzer Batt.	22/06/1915	22/06/1915
War Diary	Ypres Railway Wood (Ypres. Roulers Ry)	01/07/1915	06/07/1915
War Diary	C.R.A	07/07/1915	22/08/1915
War Diary	A 1 Trench	26/08/1915	07/09/1915
Heading	29th Trench Mortar Bty Sheet B Complete Vol I Jan Vol I		
War Diary	Trenches Infantry Field	07/01/1916	10/01/1916
Heading	Y 50 Trench Mortar Bty Late 29 T M Bde Vol III		
War Diary	I 22 Central		

War Diary	I 30 a 8.4	06/03/1916	31/03/1916
Heading	Z 50 TM Bty Vol IV I		
War Diary	N 18 C	02/04/1916	30/04/1916
War Diary	Q 28.d.17	01/05/1916	25/05/1916
War Diary	Sheet 28 N 18 C	26/05/1916	31/05/1916
War Diary	N 17 D	01/06/1916	30/06/1916
War Diary	M.24 D 10.5	01/07/1916	25/07/1916
War Diary	N 24 a 4.4. & N 24 a 27	26/07/1916	27/07/1916
War Diary	N 24 a 4.4	27/07/1916	27/07/1916
War Diary	M 24.a. 4.4	28/07/1916	30/07/1916
War Diary	N.18d. 7.3	01/07/1916	31/07/1916
War Diary	N.18d. 7.3	15/07/1916	30/07/1916
War Diary	Sheet 28. M.18.d 8.6	01/08/1916	09/08/1916
War Diary	Sheet 27 Q.20.a.1.8	09/08/1916	11/08/1916
War Diary	Bois Berques	12/08/1916	12/08/1916
Miscellaneous	On His Majesty's Service.		
War Diary	Sheet 28 B. 15.a.2.7	01/12/1917	10/12/1917
War Diary	G.15.a	11/12/1917	12/12/1917
War Diary	G.10.c.1.4.	13/12/1917	18/12/1917
War Diary	G.10.c14.	19/12/1917	21/12/1917
War Diary	G.1.b.4.8	22/12/1917	28/12/1917
War Diary	I.8.d.1.8.	29/12/1917	31/12/1917
War Diary	Sheet 28. I 8.d.1.8	01/01/1918	07/01/1918
War Diary	G.7.b.4.8	08/01/1918	13/01/1918
War Diary	Hardifort	14/01/1918	14/01/1918
War Diary	Renescure	15/01/1918	15/01/1918
War Diary	Ouve Wirquin	16/01/1918	27/01/1918
War Diary	Renescure	28/01/1918	28/01/1918
War Diary	Hardifort	29/01/1918	29/01/1918
War Diary	Poperinghe	30/01/1918	30/01/1918
War Diary	I.4.a.6.8	31/01/1918	22/02/1918
War Diary	Hardifort	23/02/1918	23/02/1918
War Diary	Ouve Wirquin	24/02/1918	28/02/1918
Heading	50th (Northumbrian) Artillery. 50th Divisional Trench Mortars March 1918		
War Diary	Ouve Wirquin	01/03/1918	08/03/1918
War Diary	Thennes	09/03/1918	12/03/1918
War Diary	Chuignolles	13/03/1918	15/03/1918
War Diary	Buire	16/03/1918	22/03/1918
War Diary	Faucaucourt	23/03/1918	23/03/1918
War Diary	Chuignolles	24/03/1918	25/03/1918
War Diary	Hamel	26/03/1918	26/03/1918
War Diary	Marcelcave	27/03/1918	27/03/1918
War Diary	Boves	28/03/1918	28/03/1918
War Diary	Sourdon	29/03/1918	29/03/1918
War Diary	Boves	30/03/1918	31/03/1918
Heading	50th Divisional Trench Mortar Batteries April 1918		
War Diary	Boves	01/04/1918	04/04/1918
War Diary	Sains-Les-Amienois	05/04/1918	09/04/1918
War Diary	Du-Pont-De-Metz	10/04/1918	10/04/1918
War Diary	Domqueur	11/04/1917	11/04/1917
War Diary	Blangerval	12/04/1918	12/04/1918
War Diary	Tangry	13/04/1918	13/04/1918
War Diary	St. Hilaire	14/04/1918	14/04/1918
War Diary	Lapugnoy	15/04/1918	15/04/1918
War Diary	Oblinghem	16/04/1918	25/04/1918

War Diary	Nedon	26/04/1918	30/04/1918
War Diary	Berry Au Bac No. 0	01/05/1918	27/05/1918
War Diary	Courjodnet	01/06/1918	03/06/1918
War Diary	Near Laghy	03/06/1918	03/06/1918
War Diary	Near Laghy	03/06/1918	23/06/1918
War Diary	Verdey	24/06/1918	30/06/1918
War Diary	Verdey (Marne)	01/07/1918	05/07/1918
War Diary	Bettencourt-Riviere (Somme)	27/07/1918	28/07/1918
War Diary	Eccart Farm	29/07/1918	31/07/1918
War Diary	Verdey (Marne)	01/07/1918	04/07/1918
War Diary	Bettencourt-Riviere (Somme)	05/07/1918	28/07/1918
War Diary	Eccart Farm	27/07/1918	31/07/1918
War Diary		01/08/1918	31/08/1918
War Diary		01/09/1918	01/09/1918
War Diary		01/10/1918	31/10/1918
War Diary	Montay	01/11/1918	30/11/1918
War Diary		01/12/1918	28/12/1918
War Diary	Gommegnies	01/01/1919	31/01/1919

2

WO95/2820

50 Div

Div Trench Mortar Batteries

Aug '15 – Jan '19

50TH DIVISION

TRENCH MORTAR BATTS.

~~JAN 1916~~-JAN 1919

1915 AUG

X 50 Trench Mortar
date. 31 Bty

Vol III

L.

Army Form C. 2118

Instructions regarding War Diaries and Intelligence Summaries are contained in F. S. Regs., Part II. and the Staff Manual respectively. Title Pages will be prepared in manuscript. 31st Trench Battery

WAR DIARY
or
INTELLIGENCE SUMMARY
(Erase heading not required.)

31st Trench [illegible] Bty

Place	Date	Hour	Summary of Events and Information	Remarks and references to Appendices
	16-8-15		Attached to 150 Infantry Brigade Battery Resting	
	17-8-15		Battery Resting	
	18-8-15		O.C. reconnoitred positions for guns in Trenches 67 & 70	
	19-8-15		Put guns into Action in Trenches 67 & 70	
	20-8-15		Fired 8 light bombs from Trench 70, having two Blind, remainder were good shots. put a gun in 72 Trench	
	21-8-15		Fired 1 light bomb from Trench 67 which was + by about 15x. Shifted gun from 72 Trench to 74 for a special work.	
	22-8-15		Paid out. Fired 20 Heavy Bombs at 5pm in Trench 74, creating considerable damage to an enemy Redoubt	

[initials] 24/8/15

A S Walker 2/Lt RA
O.C. 31st Trench Battery

1875 Wt. W593/826 1,000,000 4/15 J.B.C. & A. A.D.S.S./Forms/C. 2118.

Instructions regarding War Diaries and Intelligence Summaries are contained in F. S. Regs., Part II. and the Staff Manual respectively. Title Pages will be prepared in manuscript. 31st Trench Battery

WAR DIARY
or
INTELLIGENCE SUMMARY
(Erase heading not required.)

Army Form C. 2118

31st T M Bty

Place	Date	Hour	Summary of Events and Information	Remarks and references to Appendices
Armentieres	23.8.15		Removed gun from 74 Trench to 76 Trench for special work.	
	24.8.15		Fired 18 bombs from 76 Trench, having 8 blind and 4 premature. Fired 5 Bombs from 67 Trench having 2 blind. The other 3 rounds damaging the enemy parapets & wire	
	25/8/15		Fired 4 rounds in 67 Trench having 1 Blind	
	26/8/15		Lieut W. G. Cope admitted to Hospital.	
	27/8/15		Tried fired 6 Bombs from Gun lent by 2nd Army Workshops. Received 50 Heavy & 50 Light Bombs.	
	28/8/15		No firing	
	29/8/15		Fired 2 bombs from Trench 72. Both were blind.	

K 1/9/15

A. S. Walker 2/Lt. R.A.
O.C. 31st Trench Battery

1875 Wt. W593/826 1,000,000 4/15 J.B.C. & A. A.D.S.S./Forms/C. 2118.

Instructions regarding War Diaries and Intelligence Summaries are contained in F. S. Regs., Part II. and the Staff Manual respectively. Title Pages will be prepared in manuscript.

WAR DIARY
or
INTELLIGENCE SUMMARY
(Erase heading not required.)

Army Form C. 2118

31st Trench Battery.

31st T. M. Bty

Place	Date	Hour	Summary of Events and Information	Remarks and references to Appendices
	30-8-15		Fired six 3.7" Bombs from Trench 67 all were good Bursts.	
			18 par bomb 2 1st Into a working party thereby dispersing them	
			1 bomb from Trench 72 which burst on the parados.	
	31-8-15		No firing Generals orders that we were not to fire unless fired upon.	
	1-9-15		From Trench 67 three 18 par bombs which were all Blind	
			From Trench 70 1 hit in the middle of a working party, the other two were blind	
	2-9-15		From Trench 67 three 3.7" bombs, one fell in the wire the other two were blind.	
			one 18 par from 4/2 which was Blind	
	3-9-15		No firing. Put 1½ gun in position in Trench 71	
	4-9-15		Trench 67 3.7" fired 6 bombs having three blind all hitting the target	
			one 18 par from 67 which burst in Trench.	8/9/15
	5-9-15		3 Bombs from 72 Trench 3.7" one blind, the other two were effective	
			From Trench 67 two 18 par both plus but good bursts	
			Trench 67 3.7" four Bombs two of which were blind the other two bursting	
			with good effect	
			A. S. Walker 2/Lt R.A.	
			O.C. 31 Trench Bty.	

1875 Wt. W593/826 1,000,000 4/15 J.B.C. & A. A.D.S.S./Forms/C. 2118.

Army Form C. 2118

Instructions regarding War Diaries and Intelligence Summaries are contained in F. S. Regs., Part II and the Staff Manual respectively. Title Pages will be prepared in manuscript.

WAR DIARY

or

INTELLIGENCE SUMMARY

(Erase heading not required.)

Place	Date	Hour	Summary of Events and Information	Remarks and references to Appendices

1875 Wt. W593/826 1,000,000 4/15 J.B.C. & A. A.D.S.S./Forms/C. 2118.

Instructions regarding War Diaries and Intelligence Summaries are contained in F. S. Regs., Part II. and the Staff Manual respectively. Title Pages will be prepared in manuscript.

WAR DIARY
or
INTELLIGENCE SUMMARY
(Erase heading not required.)

Army Form C. 2118

Place	Date	Hour	Summary of Events and Information	Remarks and references to Appendices
	9.9.15		3.7" Gun from Trench 70 five of which dropped in the wire, one blind & one parapet. Owing to a strong headwind we could not reach the Target	
	10-9-15		From Trench 71 five 18lb bombs two of which were blind, the others were all in the Trench	
	~~10-9-15~~		From Trench 71 3.7" Gun, again the wind was against us we fired 10 bombs. 3 of which fell in the wire, 2 were Blind one of which fell on the Target, the others only fell short. Later in the evening we fired again 2 of which dropped on the parapet and one on the parados.	
			From Trench 70 fired 4 18pd bombs. one fell on the Target two were blind and the other fell on the parados. These were fired in retaliation to two 'Sausage' machines. Four Sausages were fired over two of which were blind the other two fell short.	
	11-9-15		3.7" Gun We fired 8 bombs from Trench 71 1st burst in air over the Trench 2nd fell to the Right owing to the wind 3rd direct hit, 4th to the Right 5th Burst in the air. The Germans put over two Sausages. We fired in retaliation one of which fell on the parapet one burst in the wire the other burst in The air.	20/9/15

1875 Wt. W593/826 1,000,000 4/15 J.B.C. & A. A.D.S.S./Forms/C. 2118.

Instructions regarding War Diaries and Intelligence Summaries are contained in F. S. Regs., Part II. and the Staff Manual respectively. Title Pages will be prepared in manuscript.

WAR DIARY

or

INTELLIGENCE SUMMARY

(Erase heading not required.)

Army Form C. 2118

31st T.M. Bty

Place	Date	Hour	Summary of Events and Information	Remarks and references to Appendices
	[illegible].9.15		Fired two 15 pdr bombs from trenches 71 & 72. Both [illegible] direct hits in the N trench.	

A.S. Walker 2/Lt R.G.A.
O.C. 31st Trench Batty.

20/9/15

1875 Wt. W593/826 1,000,000 4/15 J.B.C. & A. A.D.S.S./Forms/C. 2118.

Army Form C. 2118

WAR DIARY
or
INTELLIGENCE SUMMARY
(Erase heading not required.)

Instructions regarding War Diaries and Intelligence Summaries are contained in F. S. Regs., Part II. and the Staff Manual respectively. Title Pages will be prepared in manuscript.

31st Trench Battery

31st T. M. Bty

Place	Date	Hour	Summary of Events and Information	Remarks and references to Appendices
	13-9-15	9.30am	From 67 fired 3 18pd bombs at a working party which were dispersed one was Blind	
		11am	From 71 fired 6 4pd. bombs ~~all were~~ two Burst in the air the remainder were effective in the Trench	
			From 71 fired one 18pd. Bomb which fell in the Trench, the Huns replied with two Sausages We replied from Trenches 71 & 70 with two rounds each having one blind. The Huns again replied with two Sausages one Blind We again fired from 70 & 71 having one Blind. The Huns put two more Sausages over which were both blind We replied with a round from 70, 71 & 72 two were effective & one Blind We replied with one from 70 which was Blind The five Sausages which burst were all well short of our wire.	
	14-9-15		Fired 8 bombs in retaliation to four Sausages	
	15-9-15		Fired 4 bombs "	
	16-9-15	11am	Fired one from Trench 70 at a working party which was dispersed	
		3pm	Fired one from Trench 70, 71 & 72 in reply to a Sausage	
	17-9-15		No firing	
	18-9-15		Fired two bombs from Trench 70 having one blind the other was effective From Trench 72 fired 1 bomb. which blew up a dugout From Trench 71 fired 3 bombs having 2 duds the other one apparently blowing up a dugout.	

1875 Wt. W593/826 1,000,000 4/15 J.B.C. & A. A.D.S.S./Forms/C. 2118.

Instructions regarding War Diaries and Intelligence Summaries are contained in F. S. Regs., Part II. and the Staff Manual respectively. Title Pages will be prepared in manuscript.

WAR DIARY

or

INTELLIGENCE SUMMARY

(Erase heading not required.)

Army Form C. 2118

Place	Date	Hour	Summary of Events and Information	Remarks and references to Appendices

1875 Wt. W593/826 1,000,000 4/15 J.B.C. & A. A.D.S.S./Forms/C. 2118.

Army Form C. 2118

Instructions regarding War Diaries and Intelligence Summaries are contained in F. S. Regs., Part II. and the Staff Manual respectively. Title Pages will be prepared in manuscript.

WAR DIARY
or
INTELLIGENCE SUMMARY
(Erase heading not required.)

31st Trench Battery

31st Trench Mortar Bty

Place	Date	Hour	Summary of Events and Information	Remarks and references to Appendices
	20-9-15	11 pm	From Trench 74 fired eight Heavy Bombs at the Black Redoubt all of which were effective, 1st & 2nd rounds fell in the Trench, the 3rd apparently blew a dug-out up as Timber was seen in the air. The 4th also blew a dug out up as Timber & what appeared to be a man's body was seen in the air. The remaining rounds were all direct hits on the Redoubt.	
		4 pm	From Trench 72 fired 6 Light Bombs having one Blind the remaining five burst with good effect in the Trench, these were fired in retaliation to Whizz Bangs. The 5th round dropped on a dug out and blew it up. Clothes, Timber & Corrugated Iron were seen.	
	21-9-15		Fired one bomb from Trench 70 in retaliation to six Rifle Grenades	
			From Trench 71 fired three bombs two of which were duds the third dropped in the trench.	
	22-9-15		No firing	K 29/9/15
	23-9-15		No firing	
	24-9-15		Ordered to bring guns out of action	
	25-9-15		Battery Resting	
	26-9		—	

A. G. Walker 2/Lt. R.F.A.
O.C. 31 Trench Bty

1875 Wt. W593/826 1,000,000 4/15 J.B.C. & A. A.D.S.S./Forms/C. 2118.

Army Form C. 2118.

Instructions regarding War Diaries and Intelligence Summaries are contained in F. S. Regs., Part II. and the Staff Manual respectively. Title pages will be prepared in manuscript.

WAR DIARY

or

INTELLIGENCE SUMMARY.

(Erase heading not required.)

Place	Date	Hour	Summary of Events and Information	Remarks and references to Appendices

1577 Wt. W10791/1773 500,000 1/15 D. D. & L. A.D.S.S./Forms/C. 2118.

WAR DIARY
or
INTELLIGENCE SUMMARY.
(Erase heading not required.)

Army Form C. 2118.

Instructions regarding War Diaries and Intelligence Summaries are contained in F. S. Regs., Part II. and the Staff Manual respectively. Title pages will be prepared in manuscript.

(Cont) 31st Trench Mortar Bty

Place	Date	Hour	Summary of Events and Information	Remarks and references to Appendices
Littlefield	16-11-17	9am	Route March 3pm Rifle & Bayonet Inspection	
Sheet 27	17-11-17	---	Swedish Drill 11am Squad Drill 3pm Lecture on Telephony	
W19 a 38	18-11-17	--	Route March 11-30am Semaphore 3pm Football Match.	
	19-11-17	--	Church Parade Kit Inspection.	
	20-11-17	--	Route March 11-15am Semaphore 3pm Swedish Drill	
	21-11-17	--	Baths 3pm Fatigues for 50th D.A.C.	
	22-11-17	--	Route March 3pm Football Match Battery visited by Commandant Trench Mortar Bde	
	23-11-17	--	Kit & Rifle Inspection 11am Working Party for D.A.C. 3pm party for D.A.C.	
	24-11-17	--	Route March 3pm Semaphore.	
	25-11-17	--	Route March 3pm ~~[illegible]~~	
	26-11-17	--	Route March	
	27-11-17	--	Squad Drill 11am Semaphore 3pm Rifle Inspection & Swedish Drill.	
	28-11-17	--	1 N.C.O. detailed to proceed to Bombing School 3pm Gun Drill.	
	29-11-17		Route March ~~Battery was visited by Commandant Trench Mortar Brigade~~	
	30-11-17	10am	Inspection by General Plumer. 3pm Swedish Drill & Lecture on Telephony.	

Bernard Henderson 2Lt East Yorks
for O.C. 31 T M Bty

1577 Wt. W10791/1773 500,000 1/15 D. D. & L. A.D.S.S./Forms/C. 2118.

Instructions regarding War Diaries and Intelligence Summaries are contained in F. S. Regs., Part II. and the Staff Manual respectively. Title pages will be prepared in manuscript.

3rd Trench Morta. Bty

WAR DIARY
or
INTELLIGENCE SUMMARY.
(Erase heading not required.)

31st Trench Mortar Battery

Army Form C. 2118.

Place	Date	Hour	Summary of Events and Information	Remarks and references to Appendices
Sheet 27	1-12-16	9am	Lecture on Bombing 11-30 Semaphore	
W19a38.	2-12-16		Route March 2pm Semaphore	
	3-12-16		Bathing parade 2pm Gun Drill.	
	4-12-16		Route March 11-30am Squad Drill	
	5-12-16		Church Parade & Kit Inspection	
	6-12-16		Route March 11am Semaphore 2pm Gun Drill.	
	7-12-16		Route March 11am Squad Drill 2pm Swedish Drill.	
	8-12-16		Route March 11a Semaphore 2pm Squad Drill.	
	9-12-16		Baths 2pm Squad Drill	
	10-12-16		Squad Drill 11am Gun Drill 2pm Semaphore.	
	11-12-16		Gun Drill 11am Squad Drill	
	12-12-16		Church Parade & Kit Inspection	
	13-12-16		Route March Semaphore 2pm Squad Drill.	
	14-12-16		Squad Drill 11am Semaphore 2pm Swedish Drill & Telephony.	
	15-12-16		Fatigues 11am Inspection by Commandant Trench Mortar Bde 2-3 A.R.A.(?)	
	16-12-16		Bath.	

[initials] 11/1/1[illegible]

1577 Wt. W10791/1773 500,000 1/15 D. D. & L. A.D.S.S./Forms/C. 2118.

WAR DIARY
or
INTELLIGENCE SUMMARY.
(*Erase heading not required.*)

Army Form C. 2118.

Instructions regarding War Diaries and Intelligence Summaries are contained in F. S. Regs., Part II. and the Staff Manual respectively. Title pages will be prepared in manuscript.

31st French Mortar Bty

Place	Date	Hour	Summary of Events and Information	Remarks and references to Appendices
Sheet 27.	17.12.15	9am	Route March 11-30am Squad Drill.	Ky 1/1/16
W19a 38.	18.12.15	---	Route March 11-30am Semaphore.	
	19.12.15	3pm	Moved to new billets arriving at 8-30pm Map Position Sheet 28 G28 a 1.1	
Hill 60. Sheet 28 N.W. I29 6 80.	20.12.15		Rained nearly all day Everything very quiet. Orders not to fire until reliefs were well through. Reported to O.C. 5th N.F. re. new dug out – The R.E. are going to build one Took an inventory of stores etc left things were in a very bad condition owing to having been buried in the dug-out	
	21.12.15		Took one Section of the Battery into the trenches We were shelled fairly heavily on the way up	
	22.12.15		Rained nearly all day Orders to Strafe I29 a 3.7 On Saturday cleaned all guns and stores	
	23.12.15		Started 2" emplacement behind 38 S and attended to emplacement behind 40 & 41 Sent orderly to O.C. 33rd Battery re Strafe	
	24.12.15		Very quiet all day Worked on the two positions in morning then received wire postponing shoot. Worked in Communication Trench which had fallen in at 6-15pm we called on to fire (I 38) the emplacement was flooded, pulled out the bed	

Instructions regarding War Diaries and Intelligence Summaries are contained in F. S. Regs., Part II. and the Staff Manual respectively. Title pages will be prepared in manuscript.

WAR DIARY
or
INTELLIGENCE SUMMARY.
(Erase heading not required.)

Army Form C. 2118.

Place	Date	Hour	Summary of Events and Information	Remarks and references to Appendices

1577 Wt. W10791/1773 500,000 1/15 D. D. & L. A.D.S.S./Form/C. 2118.

Army Form C. 2118.

Instructions regarding War Diaries and Intelligence Summaries are contained in F. S. Regs., Part II. and the Staff Manual respectively. Title pages will be prepared in manuscript.

WAR DIARY
or
INTELLIGENCE SUMMARY.
(Erase heading not required.)

31 Trench Mortar Bty.

Place	Date	Hour	Summary of Events and Information	Remarks and references to Appendices
Hill 60.	30-12-15		ceased firing. They were fitted with old pattern fuzes.	
Sheet 28. N.W. I29. 680	31-12-15		Working on Emplacement behind 37S. Could not work during early part of morning owing to bombardment.	[illegible] 7/1/16

A S Walker 2Lt RGA
OC. 31 TM Bty

1577 Wt. W10791/1773 500,000 1/15 D. D. & L. A.D.S.S./Forms/C. 2118.

31st Trench Mortar Bty

Jan

Vol VII

3/1st Battery
Trench Mortar Brigade
50th Division

Instructions regarding War Diaries and Intelligence Summaries are contained in F. S. Regs., Part II. and the Staff Manual respectively. Title pages will be prepared in manuscript.

WAR DIARY
or
INTELLIGENCE SUMMARY.
(Erase heading not required.)

Army Form C. 2118.

Place	Date	Hour	Summary of Events and Information	Remarks and references to Appendices
Sheet 28				
I 29 c 1.4	10-1-16		Left Section relieved by Right Section at noon. Worked on 2inch emplacement in LOVERS LANE. At 3-45 pm we called upon to fire in reply to enemy mortar. Fired two rounds from 4 inch in JOHNSONS TRENCH. Both were effective and enemy ceased fire. Called on again at 5-30 pm and fired three rounds from 4 inch gun in JOHNSONS TRENCH all were effective	
	11-1-16		Worked on 2inch emplacement in LOVERS LANE & bomb store in the CUTTING all day fixed elevating gear on bed for 2inch gun in SWITCH could not register with that gun owing to the light being so bad for observation purposes	
	12-1-16		Worked on 2inch emplacement in LOVERS LANE & Bomb store in the CUTTING all day. At 10-45am fired two rounds from 2inch gun in SWITCH to register I 29 d 5.7. First shot fell in enemy's wire the second on parados both burst & enemy replied with a rifle grenade. Had order from Brigadier to fire on exposed mine shaft I 35 A 7.9. Took up bed of 2inch gun in SWITCH and relaid it so that gun could fire on that point. Very Quiet night	
	13-1-16		Continued work on 2" emplacement in LOVERS LANE and bomb store in CUTTING. Fired 3 rounds from 2" gun in Switch on CATERPILLAR opposite 37 Trench. First fell in enemy wire the second was blind and the third was over but a considerable quantity of timber was thrown up. Moved 2inch bed so that gun could fire on I 29 d 3.7.	

1577 Wt. W10791/1773 500,000 1/15 D. D. & L. A.D.S.S./Forms/C. 2118.

Army Form C. 2118

Instructions regarding War Diaries and Intelligence Summaries are contained in F. S. Regs., Part II. and the Staff Manual respectively. Title Pages will be prepared in manuscript.

WAR DIARY

or

INTELLIGENCE SUMMARY

(Erase heading not required.)

Place	Date	Hour	Summary of Events and Information	Remarks and references to Appendices

1875 Wt. W593/826 1,000,000 4/15 J.B.C. & A. A.D.S.S./Forms/C. 2118.

Instructions regarding War Diaries and Intelligence Summaries are contained in F. S. Regs., Part II. and the Staff Manual respectively. Title Pages will be prepared in manuscript.

WAR DIARY
or
INTELLIGENCE SUMMARY
(Erase heading not required.)

Army Form C. 2118

Place	Date	Hour	Summary of Events and Information	Remarks and references to Appendices
	19-1-16		At 1.30 pm opened fire on I 29 d 3.7 with 2 inch gun in SWITCH. Fired 6 rounds, the first falling short in the wire, the second was blind, the third fourth fifth sixth shots were all effective doing considerable damage. The fourth round apparently struck a dug-out as a great deal of timber was seen in the air also what appeared to be part of a man's body or clothing. At 5.15 pm sent 1 N.C.O + 6 men to collect 3.7 gun bed. Quiet night.	
	20-1-16		Continued work on 2 inch emplacement in LOVERS LANE + bomb store in CUTTING. Fixed new 2 inch bed in position in SWITCH. Received orders from O C 6th NF to fire 10 rounds at 3 pm. Opened fire from 1½ inch gun in JOHNSONS TRENCH + fired one round which was blind. Fired 9 rounds from 2 inch gun in JOHNSONS TRENCH. The first five burst effectively in the enemy trench + judging by the amount of timber thrown up after the fifth round it must have dropped on a dug-out or heap of timber. The sixth round was blind. The remainder all burst effectively in the enemy trench. The last did a considerable amount of damage. The enemy replied with a few "whizz bangs". Quiet night.	
	21-1-16		Continued work on 2 inch emplacement in LOVERS LANE + bomb store in CUTTING. Received orders to fire 10 rounds from 1½ inch gun in JOHNSONS TRENCH. Opened fire at 11.45 am with 18 pdr bombs. The first two fell short in their wire the third + fourth in their trench doing a fair amount of damage. After the fourth round the Huns began to drop sausages over + one fell behind our observation post. I ceased fire + found a new point from which to observe. We again opened fire + all bombs burst effectively in their trench + parados. The last three bombs did considerable amount of damage. Ceased fire owing to shortage of ammunition. At 5.15 pm fired my last 2 rounds	

1875 Wt. W593/826 1,000,000 4/15 J.B.C. & A. A.D.S.S./Forms/C. 2118.

Instructions regarding War Diaries and Intelligence Summaries are contained in F. S. Regs., Part II and the Staff Manual respectively. Title Pages will be prepared in manuscript.

WAR DIARY
or
INTELLIGENCE SUMMARY
(Erase heading not required.)

Army Form C. 2118

Place	Date	Hour	Summary of Events and Information	Remarks and references to Appendices

1875 Wt W503/826 1,000,000 4/15 J.B.C. & A. A.D.S.S./Forms/C. 2118.

Army Form C. 2118

WAR DIARY
or
INTELLIGENCE SUMMARY
(Erase heading not required.)

Instructions regarding War Diaries and Intelligence Summaries are contained in F. S. Regs., Part II. and the Staff Manual respectively. Title Pages will be prepared in manuscript.

Place	Date	Hour	Summary of Events and Information	Remarks and references to Appendices
	25-1-16		& sausages. The enemy were still persistent, so fired 7 rounds from 1½" gun in Trench 40/41 on I 29 d 3.7. This silenced the Hun for the remainder of the night.	
	26-1-16		Continued work on 2 inch emplacement in LOVERS LANE & completed bomb store in CUTTING. At 1pm sent 2 men to bomb store KRUISSTRAAT to exchange 6 fuzes in accordance with instructions received from O.C. 50th Divl Trench Mortar Bgde. Received 20 rounds 60 pdr & 13 rounds 18 pdr. One Sergeant & two other ranks came up for instruction. Between 7pm & midnight fired 19 rounds from 1½" gun in Trench 40/41 on I 29 d 3.7 in retaliation for rifle grenades & sausages.	
	27-1-16		Continued work on 2 inch emplacement in LOVERS LANE. Transferred ammunition from old bomb store to new one in CUTTING. Quiet night.	
	28-1-16		Continued work on 2 inch emplacement in LOVERS LANE. Commenced officers dugout behind DUMP. At 11am opened fire with 2 inch gun in SWITCH on I 29 d 3.7 Fired 12 rounds. Two were blind, but the remainder all did damage to the Hun trenches. He replied with sausages. At 7.30 pm fired 6 rounds from 1½ inch gun & 1 round from 4 inch gun in JOHNSON'S TRENCH in retaliation for rifle grenades & sausages over Tr. 39.	
	29-1-16		Continued work on 2 inch emplacement in LOVERS LANE & dugout behind DUMP. At 5.30pm fired 7 rounds from 1½ inch gun in JOHNSON'S TRENCH on HILL 60 in retaliation for rifle grenades. Asked by O.C. 5th N.F. to fire on I 29 d 3.7 Fired 5 rounds from 2" gun in SWITCH.	
	30-1-16		Continued work on 2 inch emplacement in LOVERS LANE & dugout behind DUMP. At 9.30am fired 8 rounds from 4 inch gun in JOHNSON'S TRENCH on HILL 60 & 1 round from 2 inch gun in SWITCH on I 29 d 3.7, in retaliation for rifle grenades. Between 7 & 8pm fired 5 rounds from 2" gun in SWITCH on I 29 d 3.7, 5 rounds from 4" gun & 3 rounds from 1½ inch gun in JOHNSON'S TRENCH in retaliation for rifle grenades.	
	31-1-16		At 7am fired 7 rounds from 4" gun & 6 rounds from 1½" gun in JOHNSON'S TRENCH in retaliation for rifle grenades. All were effective, one shot falling on a dugout where cooking was evidently in progress. Right section relieved Right Section at 11am.	

[illegible] II Lt
O.C. 31st Battery
Trench Mortar Bgde
50th Div

1875 Wt. W593/826 1,000,000 4/15 J.B.C. & A. A.D.S.S./Forms/C. 2118.

TA

31 Trench Mortar Bty

X. 50 Feb
Vol II

1

50

Instructions regarding War Diaries and Intelligence Summaries are contained in F. S. Regs., Part II. and the Staff Manual respectively. Title pages will be prepared in manuscript.

WAR DIARY
or
INTELLIGENCE SUMMARY.
(Erase heading not required.)

Army Form C. 2118.

31st Trench Mortar Battery

Place	Date	Hour	Summary of Events and Information	Remarks and references to Appendices
I 29. c. 1-5. Sheet 28	1.2.16		Continued work on Officers dug-out all day. Opened fire on I 29 d 0.4 with 1½" gun in Johnsons trench and fired eight rounds, the first two bursting in their trench, the third on their parapet, the fourth was a blind. The fifth and sixth fell on their parados and parapet respectively, the seventh and eighth were unobserved. Had to cease firing owing to heavy mist. The enemy retaliated with a few Whizz-bangs and sausages. At 3.45 pm opened fire on the same spot with the same gun and fired six rounds, five burst effectively, the sixth was a blind.	
"	2.2.16		Finished Officers dug-out and worked on 2 inch emplacement in Lovers lane, also fixed permanent bed for 1½ inch in Johnsons trench. At 10.30 am opened fire on on I 29 d 3.7 with 2 inch gun from switch and fired 12 rounds. All except the ninth round burst effectively. The first two fell a little plus, the third was a direct hit on the mound of earth on the Dogs Tooth. The remaining rounds fell close to this spot. After the third round the enemy retaliated with some sausages a few of which were duds. At 11.45 am opened fire on I 29. d. 0.4. with 1½" gun in Johnsons trench and fired five rounds all of which did considerable damage. The second round apparently hit a dug-out as a great deal of timber was seen	

1577 Wt. W10791/1773 500,000 1/15 D. D. & L. A.D.S.S./Forms/C. 2118.

Instructions regarding War Diaries and Intelligence Summaries are contained in F. S. Regs., Part II. and the Staff Manual respectively. Title pages will be prepared in manuscript.

WAR DIARY

or

INTELLIGENCE SUMMARY.

(Erase heading not required.)

Army Form C. 2118.

Place	Date	Hour	Summary of Events and Information	Remarks and references to Appendices

1577 Wt. W10791/1773 500,000 1/15 D. D. & L. A.D.S.S./Forms/C. 2118.

Instructions regarding War Diaries and Intelligence Summaries are contained in F. S. Regs., Part II. and the Staff Manual respectively. Title pages will be prepared in manuscript.

WAR DIARY
or
INTELLIGENCE SUMMARY.
(Erase heading not required.)

Army Form C. 2118.

31st Trench Mortar Battery

Place	Date	Hour	Summary of Events and Information	Remarks and references to Appendices
I29.c.1.5 Sheet 28.			37 trench. Finished 1½" emplacement in the afternoon and fixed gun into position. It was too dark to register. At 11.45 pm fired five rounds from 1½" gun in Johnson's trench on to I 29 d 0.4. All the bombs burst effectively.	
"	6.2.16		Worked all day on 2" emplacement in Lovers Lane. Registered 1½" gun behind 37 trench. Fired three rounds. At 2 pm fired 7 rounds in retaliation to enemy mortars. Fired on I 29 d. 0.4 all bombs bursting effectively in their trench doing considerable damage. Left section relieved right section at 4.30 pm. Quiet night.	
"	7.2.16		Continued work on 2" emplacement off Lovers Lane. At 5.15 pm opened fire on I 29. d. 3.7. with 2" gun in switch in the hopes of catching a working party. Fired five rounds all of which burst effectively. The enemy retaliated with whizz-bangs. Quiet night. Cpl Latter sent to hospital with contusion of toe.	
"	8.2.16		Continued work on 2" emplacement in Lovers Lane. At 5.15 pm fired 4 rounds from 1½" gun in Johnson's trench on to Hill 60 in retaliation for rifle grenades. Took bearing of flash of Whizz-bang gun which was firing	

1577 Wt. W10791/1773 500,000 1/15 D. D. & L. A.D.S.S./Forms/C. 2118.

Instructions regarding War Diaries and Intelligence Summaries are contained in F. S. Regs., Part II. and the Staff Manual respectively. Title pages will be prepared in manuscript.

WAR DIARY
or
INTELLIGENCE SUMMARY.
(Erase heading not required.)

Army Form C. 2118.

Place	Date	Hour	Summary of Events and Information	Remarks and references to Appendices

1577 Wt. W10791/1773 500,000 1/15 D. D. & L. A.D.S.S./Forms/C. 2118.

Instructions regarding War Diaries and Intelligence Summaries are contained in F. S. Regs., Part II. and the Staff Manual respectively. Title pages will be prepared in manuscript.

WAR DIARY
or
INTELLIGENCE SUMMARY.
(Erase heading not required.)

Army Form C. 2118.

31st Trench Mortar Battery

Place	Date	Hour	Summary of Events and Information	Remarks and references to Appendices
I 29. C. 1. 5. Sheet 28.			Johnson's trench and two rounds at 5.30 am from same gun in retaliation for rifle grenades.	
"	12.2.16		Continued work on 2" emplacement in Lovers lane and dug-out in Johnsons trench. Received 36 rounds 18 pdr ammunition.	
"	13.2.16		Continued work on 2" emplacement off Lovers Lane and dug-out in Johnson's trench. At 7 pm fired 3 rounds (18 pdr) from 1½" gun in 40/41 trenches. Enemy evidently had that gun marked as they put three trench mortar bombs within a few feet of it. Fired 5 rounds (33 pdr) from 1½" gun in 37 trench and 12 rounds (18 pdr) from 1½" gun in Johnson's trench in retaliation for trench mortar bombs.	
"	14.2.16		Detachment under Lieut Gibson relieved by detachment under Lieut Barron.	
		11 pm	Fired 6 rounds (18 pdr) from 1½" gun in Johnsons trench on enemy trenches from I 29 c 8, 1, to I 29, d, 0.4. in retaliation for trench mortar bombs and rifle grenades.	
"	15.2.16		Set working parties digging new emplacements at 37 trench, 41 S, and continuing work at emplacements off Johnsons trench and Lovers Lane.	

1577 Wt. W10791/1773 500,000 1/15 D. D. & L. A.D.S.S./Forms/C. 2118.

Army Form C. 2118.

Instructions regarding War Diaries and Intelligence Summaries are contained in F. S. Regs., Part II. and the Staff Manual respectively. Title pages will be prepared in manuscript.

WAR DIARY

or

INTELLIGENCE SUMMARY.

(Erase heading not required.)

Place	Date	Hour	Summary of Events and Information	Remarks and references to Appendices

1577 Wt. W10791/1773 500,000 1/15 D. D. & L. A.D.S.S./Forms/C. 2118.

Instructions regarding War Diaries and Intelligence Summaries are contained in F. S. Regs., Part II. and the Staff Manual respectively. Title pages will be prepared in manuscript.

WAR DIARY
or
INTELLIGENCE SUMMARY.
(Erase heading not required.)

Army Form C. 2118.

31st Trench Mortar Battery

Place	Date	Hour	Summary of Events and Information	Remarks and references to Appendices
I 29. c. 1-5 Sheet 28			trench on I 35, a, 6. 8. One 18 pdr was a blind but the remainder did considerable damage and succeeded in putting a stop to the enemy's trench mortar fire. Worked all night on 2" emplacement off Lovers Lane.	
"	20.2.16	1 pm	In retaliation for aerial torpedoes and trench mortar bombs fired 9 rounds (60 pdr) from 2" gun in Lovers Lane on enemy's trenches from I 29, d, 0.3, to I 29, d, 3.7. Succeeded in silencing enemy's trench mortars.	
"	21.2.16	noon	Detachment under Lt Darron relieved by detachment under 2/Lt Gibson	
		1.15 pm	Fired 3 rounds (32 pdr) from 1½" gun in Trench 37 & 1 round (18 pdr) from 1½" gun in JOHNSONS TRENCH in retaliation for sausages. Enemy ceased fire. Continued work on all emplacements.	
"	22.2.16		Continued work on all emplacement. Collected 3.7 gun from 23rd Batty.	
"	23.2.16		Continued work on all emplacements.	
		8.30 pm	Fired 3 rounds from 1½" gun in JOHNSONS TRENCH in retaliation for sausages.	
"	24.2.16		Continued work on emplacements.	
		3 pm	Fired 2 rounds from 2" gun in LOVERS LANE on HILL 60 to register.	

1577 Wt. W10791/1773 500,000 1/15 D. D. & L. A.D.S.S./Forms/C. 2118.

Instructions regarding War Diaries and Intelligence Summaries are contained in F. S. Regs., Part II. and the Staff Manual respectively. Title Pages will be prepared in manuscript.

WAR DIARY
or
INTELLIGENCE SUMMARY of 31st Trench Mortar Bty.

(Erase heading not required.)

Army Form C. 2118

Place	Date	Hour	Summary of Events and Information	Remarks and references to Appendices
I.29.c.1.5 Sheet 28	24.2.16		Fired 1 round from 1½" gun in Trench 27 & 3 rounds from 1½" gun in JOHNSONS TRENCH.	
	25.2.16		Continuing work on new emplacements.	
	26.2.16		Continued work on emplacements. Fired 2 rounds from 1½" gun in JOHNSONS TRENCH & 2 rounds (32 pdrs) from 1½" gun in Trench 27 in retaliation for rifle grenades.	
"	27.2.16		Continued work on emplacements. Fixed 2" gun in old 4" position in JOHNSONS TRENCH	
		1.30pm	Received wire from OC. Trench Mortar Bde [illegible] were taking place as usual tomorrow.	
"	28.2.16		Fired 3 rounds (16 pdr) from 1½" gun in JOHNSONS TRENCH, to check registration.	
"	29.2.16		Continued work on new 2 inch emplacement in JOHNSONS TRENCH all Day.	

[illegible] 2/Lt

for OC. 31st Trench Mortar Battery.

1875 Wt. W503/826 1,000,000 4/15 J.B.C. & A. A.D.S.S./Forms/C. 2118.

Instructions regarding War Diaries and Intelligence Summaries are contained in F. S. Regs., Part II. and the Staff Manual respectively. Title pages will be prepared in manuscript.

WAR DIARY
or
INTELLIGENCE SUMMARY. of X-50 Trench Mortar Battery

Sheet 1

Army Form C. 2118.

(Erase heading not required.)

Place	Date	Hour	Summary of Events and Information	Remarks and references to Appendices
I.29.C.3.2	1st/3/16	5.0PM	12 rounds 18 pound bombs fired on enemy trenches I 29.C.81 to I 29.d.0.4	
I 29.C 4½ 1½	...	...	22 " 33 " " " " THE CATERPILLER I 29.C.	
I.29.C.4.5.	2nd	4.32AM	5 rounds 60 " " " " HILL 60. (I 29.C.	
I 29.C.3.2	2nd	do	20 " 18 " " " " I 29.C.8.1 to I 29.d.04.	
I 29.C.4¾ 1½	2nd	do	11 " 33 " " " " I.29.C (THE CATERPILLER).	
I 29.C.5.1½	2nd	do	20 " 4 " " " " I 29.C.6½.0.	
I 29.C.4½.1	2nd	5.0	Lt Barrow (O.C. 31st (Late) T.M Battery) wounded	
	3rd	8.0AM	All Mortars and Mortar positions cleaned. All Bomb Stores re filled and bombs fuzed ready for action.	
I 29.C.4.5.	4th	8.0AM	2" position repaired.	
			1½" Mortar bed removed from I 29.C.8.7 and brought to Head Quarters, cleaned and stored.	
		11.0AM	Drained trench near our position I 29.C.3.2. Submitted to O.C. T.M Bgde. Map showing all Mortar positions and lines of fire including ranges.	
		7.0PM	Returned to T.M Bgde H.Q. One 2" Mortar, 1 damaged Newton Bed and one 4" Mortar with tool box complete. Gun crews detailed and occupied mortar positions	

T2134. Wt. W708—776. 500000. 4/15. Sir J. C. & S.

Army Form C. 2118.

Instructions regarding War Diaries and Intelligence Summaries are contained in F. S. Regs., Part II. and the Staff Manual respectively. Title pages will be prepared in manuscript.

WAR DIARY
or
INTELLIGENCE SUMMARY. of X 50 Trench Mortar Battery

(Erase heading not required.)

Place	Date	Hour	Summary of Events and Information	Remarks and references to Appendices

T2134. Wt. W708–776. 500000. 4/15. Sir J. C. & S.

Instructions regarding War Diaries and Intelligence Summaries are contained in F. S. Regs., Part II. and the Staff Manual respectively. Title pages will be prepared in manuscript.

WAR DIARY
or
INTELLIGENCE SUMMARY. of X·50 Trench Mortar Battery

(*Erase heading not required.*)

Sheet 3

Army Form C. 2118.

Place	Date	Hour	Summary of Events and Information	Remarks and references to Appendices
I.29.C.4.5.	9/3/16	2·0 PM.	Moved bed in 2" position 30° more RIGHT in order to engage target at about I.29.C.6½.0.	
I.29.C.4.5.		4.30 PM	1 round (60 pound) fired at I 29.C.6½.0. Rifle mechanism blew out and bomb dropped short into a disused CT about 100 yards behind our own FRONT LINE	
I.29.C.1.4½		4.50 PM	Defensive position started on for 2" Mortar to cover own front line from I.29.C.6½.0 to ~~I.29.d.4.8½.~~ I.29.d.1.9.	
I.29.C.4.2.		7.30 PM	3 rounds fired from STOKES GUN on TRENCHES opposite.	
I.29.C.4.5	10/3/16	8.30 AM.	8 rounds 60 pound bombs fired on I 29.C.6½.0. Considerable damage done.	
do		11.0 AM	8 " 60 " " " " do Covered way opened out	
do		3.0 PM	22 " 60 " " " " do do do do do and shaft exposed	
I.29.C.4.2		3.30 PM	2 " Stokes " " " " do.	
		10.0 PM	50 rounds 60 pound bombs collected at ZILLEBEKE STATION DUMP and conveyed to I.29.C.4.5.	
I.29.C.4.5	11/3/16	8.30 AM	9 Rounds fired at I.29.C.6½.0. More damage done. Considerable quantities of timber etc thrown up.	
I.29.C.1.4½		10.30 AM	Work on defensive position continued.	
I.29.C.1.4½	12/3/16	8.30 AM.	Work on defensive position continued and a new 1½" Mortar defensive position started on	

T2134. Wt. W708—776. 500000. 4/15. Sir J. C. & S.

Army Form C. 2118.

Instructions regarding War Diaries and Intelligence Summaries are contained in F. S. Regs., Part II. and the Staff Manual respectively. Title pages will be prepared in manuscript.

WAR DIARY
or
INTELLIGENCE SUMMARY. of X 50 Trench Mortar Battery
(Erase heading not required.)

Place	Date	Hour	Summary of Events and Information	Remarks and references to Appendices

T2131. Wt. W708–776. 500000. 4/15. Sir J. C. & S.

Instructions regarding War Diaries and Intelligence Summaries are contained in F. S. Regs., Part II. and the Staff Manual respectively. Title pages will be prepared in manuscript.

WAR DIARY
or
INTELLIGENCE SUMMARY.
(Erase heading not required.)

Army Form C. 2118.

Sheet 5
of X-50 Trench Mortar Battery.

Place	Date	Hour	Summary of Events and Information	Remarks and references to Appendices
I29.C.1.4½	17/3/16	2.0 PM	Made new O.P. at top of HILL 59. O.P. Commands HILL 60.	
do		3.0 PM.	1½" Mortar placed in position ready for defensive work	
I29.C.1.4½	18/3/16	8.30 AM.	Work continued on defensive positions and new Bomb Store started on by Field Company.	
I29.C.1.4½		9.0 PM	Received new 2" piece and rifle mechanism and put same into 2" defensive position. Position and Mortar now ready for immediate action.	
I29.c.1.4½	19/3/16	8.30 AM.	Continued work on 1½" position and strengthened 2" position	
	20/3/16	7.30 AM	Enemy sending Aerial torpedoes into area I.29.c. We retalliated on his mortar position (I29.C.9.1) from I29.C.3.2. 7 rounds 18 pound bombs fired. Silenced enemy mortar. Enemy replied with 4.2" shells on Cutting (railway) in I.29.c. and support trenches about I29.C.5.5	
		12.0 Noon.	Detachment under 2nd Lt Pakthorpe RFA relieved by detachment under Lt Hutchison.	
	20/3/16 to 21/3/16	10.30 PM to 5.0 AM	5 rounds 2" fired at I29.C.6½.0 in cooperation with our heavy artillery. Considerable damage done to enemy trenches.	
I29.C.1.4½		9.0 AM.	Continued to strengthen 2" position	
I29.C.4.5.		3.0 PM.	3 rounds 2" fired at I29.d.3.7. The first round was a premature and exploded in the position. No damage done owing to bad detonation.	The bomb tail evidently cut through the bomb and carried both detonator an fuze with it
I29.C.4.5		10.30 PM.	1 round 2" fired at I29.C.6½.0.	
I29.C.1.4½	22/3/16	9.0 AM	Continued work on Bomb Store	
I29.C.3.2		9.0 AM	" " " "	

T2134. Wt. W708—776. 500000. 4/15. Sir J. C. & S.

X. 50. T.M. Battery.

Army Form C. 2118.

WAR DIARY

~~or~~

~~INTELLIGENCE SUMMARY~~.

(Erase heading not required.)

Instructions regarding War Diaries and Intelligence Summaries are contained in F. S. Regs., Part II. and the Staff Manual respectively. Title pages will be prepared in manuscript.

Place	Date	Hour	Summary of Events and Information	Remarks and references to Appendices
The BLUFF [illegible]	23/3/16		Relieved 43rd T.M. Bty [illegible] took over [illegible] positions [illegible]	
	[illegible]		[illegible]	JOR
	[illegible]		[illegible] FIR LANE. [illegible] I [illegible] BEAN	
	[illegible]		[illegible]	
	[illegible]		[illegible] FIR LANE [illegible] a quantity of [illegible]	
	[illegible]		[illegible] 4·5" [illegible]	
			[illegible] R.A.C. 1511 [illegible] At 10 [illegible]	
			[illegible] 3 [illegible]	
	[illegible]		[illegible] FIR LANE [illegible]	
	[illegible]		[illegible] manned [illegible] from	
			[illegible] 11·0 [illegible] CRATER [illegible]	
	[illegible]		[illegible]	

T2131. Wt W708–776. 500000. 4/15. Sir J. C. & S.

X. 50. T.M. Battery.

Army Form C. 2118.

Instructions regarding War Diaries and Intelligence Summaries are contained in F. S. Regs., Part II. and the Staff Manual respectively. Title pages will be prepared in manuscript.

WAR DIARY

~~or~~

~~INTELLIGENCE SUMMARY~~

(Erase heading not required.)

Place	Date	Hour	Summary of Events and Information	Remarks and references to Appendices
The BLUFF.	30/3/16	(cont)	enemy started firing with a 'Mittlere Minenwerfer' on the LOOP trench, he fired about 10 rounds. We replied with 15 rounds Stokes, but were unable to reach him, our retaliation, however, silenced enemy.	
	31/3/16		Early this morning enemy again 'strafed' LOOP trench with two 'Minenwerfer', one suspected at O 4 b 2·8 was reported to 4·5 How^r. Battery. We fired 24 rounds and, in concert with our Howitzers, silenced the enemy. After about an hour enemy searched 31 S for us with 5·9" coal-box shrapnel, but did no damage.	
			Edward Price 2nd Lieut R.G.A (SR) actg. O.C. X.50 T.M.Bty.	

X 50 TM Bty

Vol IV

Instructions regarding War Diaries and Intelligence Summaries are contained in F. S. Regs., Part II. and the Staff Manual respectively. Title Pages will be prepared in manuscript.

WAR DIARY
or
INTELLIGENCE SUMMARY
(Erase heading not required.)

Page 1 + part of 2
of X.50 Trench Mortar Battery

Army Form C. 2118.

Place	Date	Hour	Summary of Events and Information	Remarks and references to Appendices
I.29.c.4.5.	1/4/16	7.0 PM	Canadian detachment relieved by detachment under 2nd Lt C.S. Lakthorpe R.F.A. Only one 2" Mortar in position at I 29.a.2.0	
I 29.d.6½.0	2/4/16	9.0 AM	Work started on new position at I 29.d.6½.0.	
do	3/4/16	9.0	— — do — —	
do	4/4/16	9.0	— — do — —	
do	5/4/16	9.0	— — do — —	
N.28.c.8.7.		9.0 PM	Collected material for position at I 29.d.6½.0	
	6/4/16	9.30 AM	Work ceased at I 29.d.6½.0 according to orders received from 150th Inf Brigade Major	
I 24.c.3½.7½	6/4/16	10.0 AM	New position started and put one 2" piece ready for action	
N.28.c.8.7		7.30 PM	Collected material for Mortar position	
		10.0 PM	Received orders to be prepared to open fire on I 30.a.5.7. at 10.0 AM on 7/4/16	
7/4/16	7/4/16	10.0 AM	Firing at 10.0 AM postponed till further orders. ½ hours notice only to be given	
		10.0 AM	Carried material to I 24.c.3½.7½.	
			Fuzed 60 2" bombs and conveyed ~~same~~ 30 to I 29.a.20. and 30 to I 24.c.3½.7½.	
			Tested length of time for communication between T M Batt. H.Q. + I 24.c.3½.7½. + found same to take from ¾ hours to 1½ hours. Decided to withdraw gun crew and await orders at T M Batt. H.Q.	

2449 Wt. W14957/M90 750,000 1/16 J.B.C. & A. Forms/C.2118/12.

Army Form C. 2118.

Instructions regarding War Diaries and Intelligence Summaries are contained in F. S. Regs., Part II. and the Staff Manual respectively. Title pages will be prepared in manuscript.

WAR DIARY
or
INTELLIGENCE SUMMARY. of X 50 Trench Mortar Battery
(Erase heading not required.)

Place	Date	Hour	Summary of Events and Information	Remarks and references to Appendices

T2131. Wt. W708—776. 500000. 4/15. Sir J. C. & S.

Army Form C. 2118.

3

WAR DIARY
or
INTELLIGENCE SUMMARY of X-50 Trench Mortar Battery
(Erase heading not required.)

Instructions regarding War Diaries and Intelligence Summaries are contained in F. S. Regs., Part II. and the Staff Manual respectively. Title Pages will be prepared in manuscript.

Place	Date	Hour	Summary of Events and Information	Remarks and references to Appendices
I 29.a.2.0	8/4/16	9.0 AM	Work on 2" position continued	
		10.0 AM	Received orders to put a mortar into position to fire on enemy line point N.20.a.3.8.	
I 29.a.2.0		10.15	Ceased work	
I 29.b.1.5		10.30	Started new position for 2" mortar	
		12.0 noon	Received orders to fire on point N.30.a.3.8 at 2.5 PM	
I 29.b.1.5		12.30 PM	Mortar in position. Bombs fused & carried to mortar by inf: working party & own gunners.	
		2.5 PM	Opened fire on point N.20.a.3.8.	
		2.35	18 rounds fired. Rifle mechanism jambed owing to cartridge being badly damaged. Unable to repair damage. Withdrew gun as soon as convenient. The enemy retaliated with heavy minenwerfe & whiz-bangs. Parapet in front of mortar blown ~~in~~	
I 29.b.1.5		5.0 PM	2" piece withdrawn from I 29.b.1.5	

2449 Wt. W14957/M90 750,000 1/16 J.B.C. & A. Forms/C.2118/12.

Instructions regarding War Diaries and Intelligence Summaries are contained in F. S. Regs., Part II. and the Staff Manual respectively. Title pages will be prepared in manuscript.

WAR DIARY
or
INTELLIGENCE SUMMARY. of X 50 Trench Mortar Battery

(Erase heading not required.)

Army Form C. 2118.

Place	Date	Hour	Summary of Events and Information	Remarks and references to Appendices

T2131. Wt. W708–776. 500000. 4/15. Sir J. C. & S.

A

X 50 T M Bty.

Instructions regarding War Diaries and Intelligence Summaries are contained in F. S. Regs., Part II. and the Staff Manual respectively. Title pages will be prepared in manuscript.

WAR DIARY

~~or~~

~~INTELLIGENCE SUMMARY.~~ of X·50 Trench Mortar Battery

(Erase heading not required.)

Army Form C. 2118.

Place	Date	Hour	Summary of Events and Information	Remarks and references to Appendices
N 29. c ½ 9	10/4/16	3.30pm	Detachment under 2Lt Palethorpe relieved by Detachment under 2Lt Price	
N 29. d 2·9		5.0–10.0 pm.	Work continued on gun emplacement in Pall Mall.	
N 29. c 3·8		8·0	20 rounds two-inch ammunition arrived at Regent St.	
N 29. d 2·9	11/4/16		Continued work all day on Pall Mall emplacement.	
N 24 c 3·8	12/4/16	9.30am.	Visited H I gun, and found emplacement badly damaged during night by 7·7 cm shell.	
"		11·0am	Cleaned the débris and placed T-vent in gun.	
N 30. c. 3.0	13/4/16	9·0am	Started work on new emplacement in E 3, work continued all day.	
"	14/4/16	9·0am	Continued working on E 3 position with working party (Infantry)	
N 30. a 0·7		10·0am	Started new position in G 1. continued till nightfall.	
		10–5	Deliberate shelling of C Ts by enemy 15 cm How's. 13 direct hits on Pall Mall C T.	
N 29 d. 2·9.			entrance to gun position damaged.	
	15/4/16		Work continued on all emplacements, fired 1 rd. 2" on N30·c·3·6 from E3 (N 30.c.3·0)	
	16/4/16		Enemy shelling continued all day. " 6 rds " " " " "	

T2134. Wt. W708—776. 500000. 4/15. Sir J. C. & S.

Instructions regarding War Diaries and Intelligence Summaries are contained in F. S. Regs., Part II. and the Staff Manual respectively. Title pages will be prepared in manuscript.

WAR DIARY
or
INTELLIGENCE SUMMARY. of X 50 Trench Mortar Battery

(Erase heading not required.)

Army Form C. 2118.

Place	Date	Hour	Summary of Events and Information	Remarks and references to Appendices

T2131. Wt. W708–776. 500000. 4/15. Sir J. C. & S.

Instructions regarding War Diaries and Intelligence Summaries are contained in F. S. Regs., Part II. and the Staff Manual respectively. Title pages will be prepared in manuscript.

Army Form C. 2118.

WAR DIARY
or
INTELLIGENCE SUMMARY.
(Erase heading not required.)

~~Sheet 2~~
X-50 Trench Mortar Battery

Place	Date	Hour	Summary of Events and Information	Remarks and references to Appendices.
N.29.c.3.3.	19/4/16	8.0PM	Received 20 rounds 2" (bombs) and placed same in bomb store	
N.24.C.1.5.		8.0 PM	Work ceased on new position.	
N.29.C.3.3.	20/4/16	9.0AM	20. 2" bombs, fuzed and tailed (Two new men instructed in same)	
N.24.C.1.5.		9.0AM	Work continued on new position and material prepared for bomb store.	
N.30.C.2.0		10.0AM	4 rounds 2" fired on N30.C.1.9 in Retaliation for enemy Minenwerfer bombs.	
N.29.b.2.0		11.30AM	2 " 2" " " N.30.C 1½.8 " " " " " (1 bomb was a blind).	
N.30.C.2.0		2.0 PM	Bed repaired. (Bed was damaged earlier in the day)	
N.24.C.1.5		8.0 PM	Working party arrived and built a bridge, also made parapet higher in order to obstruct enemy view from N.30.a. 3½. 2½.	
			Quiet night.	
N.24.C.1.5		9.0AM.	Bomb store under construction	
		10.0AM.	2. 2" bombs carried to position.	
		10.30AM	Prepared pieces of specially shaped canvass to be used as "Fuze Covers" for night firing in order to hide sparks from fuze during flight	
N.24.C.1.5	21/4/16	8.30AM	Work continued on position. Heavy rains stopped work	
N.24.C.1.5		4.30PM	2 rounds fired on N30. a. 5½. 8. with Good results. Damaged enemy front line & wire	

T2134. Wt. W708—776. 500000. 4/15. Sir J. C. & S.

Army Form C. 2118.

Instructions regarding War Diaries and Intelligence Summaries are contained in F. S. Regs., Part II. and the Staff Manual respectively. Title pages will be prepared in manuscript.

WAR DIARY
or
INTELLIGENCE SUMMARY. ~~[illegible]~~ of X-50 Trench Mortar Bty

(Erase heading not required.)

Place	Date	Hour	Summary of Events and Information	Remarks and references to Appendices
N24.c.1.5	22/4	8.30 pm	[illegible]	
N[illegible]		4 pm	Fired [illegible] 2" [illegible] N30.a.7.9. with good results [illegible] [illegible] [illegible]	
N29.C.3.0		4 pm	Fired [illegible] round 2" [illegible] [illegible] installation [illegible]	
N29.b.3.0	23/4	3 pm	1 round fired on N30.b.1.9 installation [illegible]	

T2131. Wt. W708—776. 500000. 4/15. Sir J. C. & S.

B

X 50 T M Bty.

Army Form C. 2118.

Instructions regarding War Diaries and Intelligence Summaries are contained in F. S. Regs., Part II. and the Staff Manual respectively. Title pages will be prepared in manuscript.

WAR DIARY ~~or~~ ~~INTELLIGENCE SUMMARY~~. of X·50 Trench Mortar Battery.

(Erase heading not required.)

Place	Date	Hour	Summary of Events and Information	Remarks and references to Appendices
N 29 c ½.9.	23/4/16	3.30 pm	Detachment under Lt Palethorpe relieved by detachment under Lt Price	
N 24 c. 2.5		5.0 pm	Fired 5 rds 2" on N 24 c. 6.1 in retalliation for 'sausages'	
N 30 c. 3.0		6.30 pm	Fired 3 rds 2" on N 30 c. 5.2 " " " minenwerfer	
N 30 c. 3.0	24/4/16	4.0 pm	Fired 8 rds 2" on " " " " "	
N 29 c. 3.8		9.0 pm	Received 20 rds 2" complete.	
N 24 c 2.5	25/4/16		Enemy trench mortars quiet, worked on G 3 B position.	
N 29 c. 3.8		9.0 pm	20 rds 2" complete came to Regent St, instead of VIA GALLIA, as arranged.	
N 30 c 3.0	26/4/16	4.0 pm	Fired 4 rds on N 30 c 3.6 in answer to minenwerfer	
N 24 c 2.5	27/4/16		Continued work on new bombstore, Enemy very quiet. Deserters report attack coming off.	
N 30 c 3.0	28/4/16		Fired 1 rd on N 30 c 5.2 during trench mortar 'Straf' by Division on our right. Owing to possible attack by enemy, all guns were manned during night as also previous night.	
N 30 c 5 2	29/4/16	10 am	Enemy delivered gas attack at 1 p.m on E trenches, 2" gun in E 3 fired 9 rounds on front line opposite. two men of detachment slightly 'gassed' owing to insufficient warning given. Gun in G 3 fired 6 rounds & then jumped loose from bed. Enemy attack failed	
N 29. c ½.9	30/4/16	3.0 pm	~~and quiet [illegible]~~. Handed over to Lieut Backhouse, 3rd Division.	

C. S. Palethorpe Lieut R.F.A
O.C. X·50 Trench M. Battery

T2134. Wt. W708—776. 500000. 4/15. Sir J. C. & S.

Instructions regarding War Diaries and Intelligence Summaries are contained in F. S. Regs., Part II. and the Staff Manual respectively. Title pages will be prepared in manuscript.

WAR DIARY
or
INTELLIGENCE SUMMARY.
(*Erase heading not required.*)

Army Form C. 2118.

X 50 TMBG

Vol 6

Place	Date	Hour	Summary of Events and Information	Remarks and references to Appendices
[illegible]	1/5/16	7.0pm	Arrived at LOCRE with relief from trenches. second relief proceeded to EECKE.	
	2/5/16	9.0am	Proceeded with remainder to EECKE.	
Q 28 d 1.7	3/5/16	9-12.30	Training, Gundrill.	
"	4/5/16	"	Training, Gun drill, telephony.	
"	5/5/16	"	Training, Signalling	
"	6/5/16	"	Fatigues	
"	7/5/16	11-30	Church parade	
"	8/5/16		Training, bed-laying, Semaphore	
"	9/5/16		Training, Gun drill.	
"	10/5/16		Training, Erecting mortar position	
"	11/5/16		Training, Telephony.	
"	12/5/16		Training, Gun drill.	
"	13/5/16		Training, Squad drill, rifle exercises	
"	14/5/16		Church Parade	
"	15/5/16		Training, Musketry.	
"	16/5/16		Training, Gun drill.	

T2131. Wt. W708—776. 500000. 4/15. Sir J. C. & S.

Instructions regarding War Diaries and Intelligence Summaries are contained in F. S. Regs., Part II. and the Staff Manual respectively. Title pages will be prepared in manuscript.

WAR DIARY

~~or~~

~~INTELLIGENCE~~ SUMMARY.

(*Erase heading not required.*)

Army Form C. 2118.

X 50 TM Bty.

Place	Date	Hour	Summary of Events and Information	Remarks and references to Appendices
Q.28 d.1.7	17/5/16	9-1230	Training, Gun drill, Semaphore.	
"	18/5/16	"	" , Instruction in use of Respirators	
"	19/5/16	"	" , Gun drill	
"	20/5/16	"	" , Fatigues.	
"	21/5/16	11.30	Church parade.	
"	22/5/16	"	Training, Musketry. Squad drill, Fatigues	
"	23/5/16		Sports, Gun drill display	
"	24/5/16		Fatigues	
	25/5/16		Proceeded to LOCRE, Detachment under 2Lt PALETHORPE proceeded to Trenches.	
	26/5/16	9.0 Am	Fatigues.	
	~~27/5/16~~	~~3.0 Pm~~		

T2134. Wt. W708-776. 500000. 4/15. Sir J. C. & S.

Instructions regarding War Diaries and Intelligence Summaries are contained in F. S. Regs., Part II. and the Staff Manual respectively. Title pages will be prepared in manuscript.

WAR DIARY
or
INTELLIGENCE SUMMARY.
(Erase heading not required.)

Army Form C. 2118.

Place	Date	Hour	Summary of Events and Information	Remarks and references to Appendices
N29 c 4.2.	26/12	7 PM	[illegible] relieved [illegible] [illegible] ammunition and [illegible]	
	28/12	9 AM	All [illegible] cleared and ammunition [illegible] in order [illegible]	
		2 PM	[illegible] all [illegible]	
N30 c 2.0		9 PM	1 Round [illegible] N30 c 4.5	
N24 [illegible]		10 AM	[illegible] N30 A.6.9 ~~N30 c [illegible]~~ [illegible] [illegible]	
N30 [illegible]		2 PM	5 [illegible] N30 A [illegible] [illegible]	
N[illegible]		4 PM	[illegible] N30 [illegible] 4.5 [illegible]	
N29 b 2.0		[illegible]	2 [illegible] N30 C 1.8 [illegible]	
N30 C 1.5		5 PM	[illegible] N30 [illegible]	
N29 [illegible]		9 PM	[illegible] N30 C 1.5	
N29 c 4.3		10 PM	[illegible] removed and put [illegible]	
N29 b [illegible]	29/12	9 AM	[illegible] stated.	
N24 [illegible]		2 PM	14 [illegible] N30 a 5.8 [illegible]	

T.2141. Wt. W708-776. 500,000. 4/15. Sir J. C. & S.

2

Army Form C. 2118.

Instructions regarding War Diaries and Intelligence Summaries are contained in F. S. Regs., Part II. and the Staff Manual respectively. Title pages will be prepared in manuscript.

WAR DIARY
or
INTELLIGENCE SUMMARY.
(Erase heading not required.)

Place	Date	Hour	Summary of Events and Information	Remarks and references to Appendices
N.30.c.2.0	29/5/16	2.30 PM	9 Rounds fired on N30.6.44 to N.30.6.5.2 in retalliation for Sausages	
		3.0 PM	5 " " " N.30.6.1.9 to N.30.6.1½.7 " " " Enemy Silenced.	
N.29.d.7½.3½.		8.0 PM	Work continued on Emplacement. Position finished and Head cover complete Bombstore partially done.	
N.29.d.7½.3½.		9.30 PM	Work Ceased on Emplacement & Bombstore	
N.29.b.7½.1½		11.0 PM	" " " " "	
N.29.d.7½.3½	30/5/16	9.0 AM	" Continued on Bombstore	
N.29.b.7½.1½		9.0 AM	" " Emplacement	
N.29.c.4.3.		7.0 PM	6 Rounds fired on N30.a.7.9 in retalliation for Sausages Enemy Silenced	
N.29.c.4.3		10.0 PM	Received 2. 2" Mortars & 20 Rounds 2" Ammn. Placed same in Bombstore.	
		11.0 PM	Work ceased on N.29.d.7½.3½ & N.29.b.7½.1½.	
N.29.b.7½.1½	31/5/16	9.0 AM	Work done on Bomb Stores	
N.29.d.7½.3½				
N.29.b.2.0.		1.30 AM	4 Rounds fired on N.30.b.1.9. to N.30.b.2.7. in retalliation for Minenwerfe Bed out of action after 4th shot. but same in order again	[illegible]
N.30.b.2.0.		11.30 AM	9 Rounds fired on N.30.b.5½.6⅞ & N.30.b.4½.4. in retalliation for Minenwerfe Shells	[illegible]

T2134. Wt. W708-776. 50000. 4/15. Sir J. C. & S.

Instructions regarding War Diaries and Intelligence Summaries are contained in F. S. Regs., Part II. and the Staff Manual respectively. Title Pages will be prepared in manuscript.

Army Form C. 2118.

WAR DIARY
or
INTELLIGENCE SUMMARY of X 50 Trench Mortar Battery.
(Erase heading not required.)

Vol 6

Place	Date	Hour	Summary of Events and Information	Remarks and references to Appendices
N 29 b. 7½. 1½ / N 29 d. 7½. 3½	1/6/16	9 am	Work continued. Quiet day.	
N 29 d. 7½. 3½ / N 29 b. 7½. 1½	2/6/16	9. am	Work continued	
N 29 b. 2. 0 / N 30 c. 8 0 / N 24 c. 1. 5.		5.30 pm	4 rounds fired on N 30. c. 1. 7. / 15 " " " N 30 c 5. 4 / 2 " " " N 30 a 5. 8. — In retaliation for minenwerfer and Sausages. Enemy silenced and enemy trenches damaged.	
N 29 b. 7½. 1½		5.30 pm	This emplacement badly damaged by enemy minenwerfer fire	
N 29. c. 4. 3		11. 0 pm	Received 100 rounds 2" Ammunition	
N 29 d. 7½. 3½.	3/6/16	9. 0 am	Mortar & ammunition placed in position ready for action	
N 30. c. 2. 0.		4 pm	5 rounds (registration) fired on N 30. c. 4¾. 3½. Enemy retaliated with minenwerfer & Sausages	
N 30. c. 2. 0		5. 0 pm	6 rounds fired in retaliation on N 30. c. 4¾. 3½. N 30. c. 5½. 6.	

2449 Wt. W14957/M90 750,000 1/16 J.B.C. & A. Forms/C.2118/12.

Army Form C. 2118.

X 50.

Instructions regarding War Diaries and Intelligence Summaries are contained in F. S. Regs., Part II. and the Staff Manual respectively. Title pages will be prepared in manuscript.

WAR DIARY
or
INTELLIGENCE SUMMARY.
(*Erase heading not required.*)

Place	Date	Hour	Summary of Events and Information	Remarks and references to Appendices
N.29.d.7½.3½	3/6/16	5.0 P.M.	6 Rounds fired in retaliation (for Minenwerfe & Sausages) on N.30.C.5.2½ & N.30.C.6.2. In the latter place a store of some kind was blown up judging by the amount of timber & boxes seen in the air after the explosion.	
			Enemy blew in our new position at N.29.b.7½.1½.	
N.29.b.2.0	4/6/16	12.45 AM	7 Rounds fired on N30.C.1.9 to N.30.C 1½.8.	
N.30.C.2.0	"	"	3 " " " N.30.C 4¾ 3½.	
N.24.C.1.5	"	"	2 " " " N30.A.6.9	
N.29.C.4.3.	"	4.0 P.M.	16 N.C.O's & men in detachment relieved by 16 N.C.O's & men	
N.29.d.7½.3½	5/6/16	9.0 AM.	Emplacement strengthened.	
N.30.C.2.0		12.0 noon	1 round fired on N30C5.4 in retaliation for 1 Minenwerfe bomb.	
N29.C.4.3.		10.0 PM	received 20 rounds 2" Ammunition.	
N29.b.2.0	6/6/16	9.0 AM.	Roof of new Bomb Store Strengthened.	
N29.d.7½.3½			Bed moved into new position and walls revetted.	
N.29.C.6.6.		4.0 PM	2nd Lt Ratsharpe relieved by 2nd Lt Rice.	
N24C.1.5		5.0	Fired three rounds in accordance with wishes of Infantry, 1 bomb fell behind our own supports.	
"		10.0 PM	Retrieved bomb	

T2134. Wt. W708–776. 500000. 4/15. Sir J. C. & S.

Army Form C. 2118.

Instructions regarding War Diaries and Intelligence Summaries are contained in F. S. Regs., Part II. and the Staff Manual respectively. Title pages will be prepared in manuscript.

WAR DIARY
or
INTELLIGENCE SUMMARY.
(Erase heading not required.)

Place	Date	Hour	Summary of Events and Information	Remarks and references to Appendices

(T4th. Wt. W.5/...-776. 500000. 4/15. Sir J. C. & S.)

Instructions regarding War Diaries and Intelligence Summaries are contained in F. S. Regs., Part II. and the Staff Manual respectively. Title pages will be prepared in manuscript.

WAR DIARY
or
INTELLIGENCE SUMMARY.
(Erase heading not required.)

X50.

Army Form C. 2118.

Place	Date	Hour	Summary of Events and Information	Remarks and references to Appendices
N24 C.1.5	14/6/16	1.0 PM	Fired 16 rounds on N.24.c.5.8 to N.24.c.6.9 } In retaliation for Minenwerfer Bombs	
N.29.d.7½.3½.	"	1.0 PM	" 15 " " N30.a.4.5 to N30.c.1.6½ } Enemy effectively silenced.	
N30.c.2.0	"	1.0 PM	" 14 " " N30.c.4.5 to N30.c.5.4 }	
		4.0 PM.	2nd Lt Price relieved by 2nd Lt [illegible]	
N.30.a.1.6½.	15/6/16	9.30 AM to 9.30 PM.	Work continued on new Emplacement & Bombstore.	
N.29.d.7½.3½.		9.30 AM to 4.0 PM	Bombstore roof Strutted & Emplacement revetted.	
N24.C.1.5	16/6/16	4.30 AM	10 Rounds fired on N.24.c.5.8.	
		5.15 AM	9 " " " N.24.c.5.8 in Retaliation for ~~[illegible]~~ Rum JARS. & Sausages	
N29b.2.0		5.30 AM	6 " " " N30.c.1.9 " " "	
N30.a.1.6½		9.30 AM to 4.0 PM	Work Continued on Emplacement & Bombstore.	
N.24.C.1.5.		7.0 PM	3 rounds fired at N24.c.6.1. for registration. Point not reached. Bed put in position to engage same	
		7.30 PM	19 Rounds fired on N.24.c.5.8 in retaliation for Rum JARS & Sausages	

T.2134. Wt. W708–776. 500000. 4/15. Sir J. C. & S.

Instructions regarding War Diaries and Intelligence Summaries are contained in F. S. Regs., Part II. and the Staff Manual respectively. Title pages will be prepared in manuscript.

WAR DIARY
or
INTELLIGENCE SUMMARY.
(Erase heading not required.)

Army Form C. 2118.

Place	Date	Hour	Summary of Events and Information	Remarks and references to Appendices

T2131. Wt W708 776. 500000. 4/15. Sir J. C. & S.

Instructions regarding War Diaries and Intelligence Summaries are contained in F. S. Regs., Part II. and the Staff Manual respectively. Title pages will be prepared in manuscript.

WAR DIARY
or
INTELLIGENCE SUMMARY.
(Erase heading not required.)

X50.

Army Form C. 2118.

Place	Date	Hour	Summary of Events and Information	Remarks and references to Appendices
N 30 a 1·6½	19/6/16		Enemy still very quiet, work continued on position	
	~~20/6/16~~	10 pm	50 bombs expected at N 28 b 6·9, nothing arrived.	
	20/6/16		50 bombs arrived N 28 b 6·9, all carried up to N 24 c 1·5	
N 24 c 1·5	21/6/16	2.0 pm	Fired 14 bombs on N 24 c 6·1 in retaliation for 'SAUSAGES'	
N 29 d 7½·3½		4.30 pm	" 5 " on N 30 c 4½·4 " " " MINENWERFERS	
N 24 c 1·5	22/6/16	8 pm	" ~~25~~ 6 " on N 24 c 5·8 " " " "	
N 29 d 7½ 3½		8 pm	" 25 " on N 30 c 4½·4 & considerable damage done to enemy trenches	
N 29 c 6·6		10·30 pm	50 rounds received ~~20~~ taken to N 29 d 7½·3½	
N 29 d 7½ 3½	23/6/16	9 pm	Enemy opened ~~intermittent~~ TM fire on all E trenches.	
"			Fired 12 rounds on N 30 c 4½ 4.	
			200 bombs arrived. 100 at N 29 c 6·6, & 100 at N 28 b 6·9. 25 taken to N 24 c 1·5, 25 to N 30 a 1·6½, 30 to N 29 b 2·0.	
			Gun in N 30 a 1·6½ got ready for action.	
N 30 a 1·6½	24/6/16	12·15 am	Opened fire on N 30 a 4½ 2½ fired 15 rounds.	
N 24 c 1·5		1·30 pm	Fired 30 rounds on N 30 a 5·8	
N 29 d 7½ 3½		5·0 pm	Fired 25 rounds on N 30 c 5·4½, 35 rds carried up from N 29 c 6·6	

T2134. Wt. W708-776. 500000. 4/15. Sir J. C. & S.

Army Form C. 2118.

Instructions regarding War Diaries and Intelligence Summaries are contained in F. S. Regs., Part II. and the Staff Manual respectively. Title Pages will be prepared in manuscript.

WAR DIARY
or
INTELLIGENCE SUMMARY

(Erase heading not required.)

Place	Date	Hour	Summary of Events and Information	Remarks and references to Appendices

2449 Wt. W14957/M90 750,000 1/16 J.B.C. & A. Forms/C.2118/12.

Army Form C. 2118.

WAR DIARY
or
INTELLIGENCE SUMMARY
(Erase heading not required.)

X 50

Instructions regarding War Diaries and Intelligence Summaries are contained in F. S. Regs., Part II. and the Staff Manual respectively. Title Pages will be prepared in manuscript.

Place	Date	Hour	Summary of Events and Information	Remarks and references to Appendices
N24.c.1.5.	27/6/16	3.0 PM	4 Rounds fired on N24.c.8½.2 in retaliation for RUM JARS. Enemy silenced	
N29.d.7½.3½	28/6/16	8.0 AM	2 " " " " " "	
N24.c.1.5.	28/6/16	10.0 AM	6 " " – N24 c.8½.2. Searching for Enemy RUM JAR Machine.	
N24.c.1.5.		12.10 PM	4 " – " do	
N29.b.2.0	29/6/16	11.0 AM	30 rounds fired on N29.c.1½.8. Retaliation for RUM JARS. Enemy line seriously damaged also dugouts.	
N29.d.7½.3½		3.0 PM	27 rounds fired on N30.c.1.6½. in retaliation for Enemy Minenwerfer Shells near our position.	
N30.a.1.6½.		5.0 PM	5 Registered on N30.a.4½.3.	
N.24.c.1.5		5.30.	24 rounds fired on. N.24.c.6.1. in retaliation for Enemy RUM JARS.	
N24.c.1.5.	30/6/16	8.0 AM	10 " " " do –	
N29.b.2.0.		11.0 AM	18 " – – N29.c.1½.8 " " " Minenwerfer Shells	
N29.d.7½.3½.			2 " – – N30.c.1.6½ " – " " " do	

H S [illegible] 2nd Lt RFA
O.C. X 50. T.M.B.

2449 Wt. W14957/M90 750,000 1/16 J.B.C. & A. Forms/C.2118/12.

Army Form C. 2118.

WAR DIARY
or
~~INTELLIGENCE~~ SUMMARY.

(Erase heading not required.)

Instructions regarding War Diaries and Intelligence Summaries are contained in F. S. Regs., Part II. and the Staff Manual respectively. Title pages will be prepared in manuscript.

August 1916 — of 50th Divisional Trench Mortar Brigade — Volume 2

Place	Date	Hour	Summary of Events and Information	Remarks and references to Appendices
Bois Bernav[illegible]	13/8/16		Marching order Inspection.	
—	14/8/16		Route march and Squad Drill.	
Sheet 62 D. [illegible]	15/8/16		Left BERNAVILLE AREA for MONTIGNY at 3.0 am. Arrived at MONTIGNY at 6.0 am.	
—	16/8/16		Route march, Squad Drill, Semaphore, Rifle Exercise, & Lectures.	
—	17/8/16		ditto	
—	18/8/16		ditto.	
—	19/8/16		ditto	
—	20/8/16		Inspection Tower Respirator, Smoke Helmet & Rifles. Church Parade	
—	21/8/16		Y.50 Battery proceeded to forward area (W.26 c.3.4 Sheet 57 D.). Route March, Gun Drill (2" & 9.45")	
—			Squad Drill, Rifle Exercise & Semaphore. Instruction in telephony.	
—	22/8/16		Squad Drill, Telephony, Semaphore, Gun Drill 2" & 9.45"; Rifle Exercise. Y. Bty in action.	
—	23/8/16		Bombing Instruction, Rifle Exercise, Squad Drill, Semaphore, Telephony.	
—	24/8/16		Route march, Bombing, Telephony, Musketry, Squad Drill.	
—	25/8/16		Bombing Instruction, Musketry on Rifle Range, Telephony, Squad Drill	
—	26/8/16		ditto.	
	27/8/16		Left MONTIGNY for forward area (W.26 c.3.4 Sheet 57 D.) by March Route at 9.0 am. Arrived at about 12 noon. Commenced erecting new camp.	

T.131. Wt. W708 776. 500,000. 4/15. Sir J. C. & S.

Army Form C. 2118.

WAR DIARY

~~or~~

~~INTELLIGENCE SUMMARY~~ of 50th DIVISIONAL TRENCH MORTAR BRIGADE.

(*Erase heading not required.*)

Instructions regarding War Diaries and Intelligence Summaries are contained in F. S. Regs., Part II. and the Staff Manual respectively. Title pages will be prepared in manuscript.

AUGUST 1916. VOLUME. 2

Place	Date	Hour	Summary of Events and Information	Remarks and references to Appendices
Sheet 57D.				
W26c3.4	28/8/16		Fatigues:- Erecting new camp. Y. Bty fired 17 rounds 2"	
— " —	29/8/16		Squad Drill, Semaphore, Rifle & Gun Drill: Fatigues, erecting new camp	
— " —	30/8/16		Squad Drill. Gun Drill, Semaphore, Rifle Exercise, etc; Parades interrupted owing to very heavy rain.	
— " —	31/8/16		Squad Drill; X. Bty fired 20 rounds 2" "THERMIT" Bombs at demonstration ~~for~~ Corps Commander, III Corps.	

W. C. Maud Capt R.A.
50th Divl Trench Mortar Officer.

50th. DIV. TRENCH MORTOR BRIGADE

S E P T E M B E R 1 9 1 6.

Vol 9 Army Form C. 2118.

Instructions regarding War Diaries and Intelligence Summaries are contained in F. S. Regs., Part II. and the Staff Manual respectively. Title pages will be prepared in manuscript.

WAR DIARY
or
INTELLIGENCE SUMMARY. of 50TH DIVISIONAL TRENCH MORTAR BRIGADE
(Erase heading not required.)

SEPTEMBER 1916 VOLUME 3

Place	Date	Hour	Summary of Events and Information	Remarks and references to Appendices
Sheet 57D.				
W26 c.3.4.	1/9/16		Route March, Gun Drill 2" & 9.45", Semaphore, Squad Drill, Rifle Exercise, Telephony, Y.50 Bty in action on Divisional Front.	
"	2/9/16		Route March, Gun Drill 2" & 9.45" & Fuze Setting. Semaphore, Squad Drill Rifle Exercise Telephony. Y.50 Battery in action on Divisional Front.	
"	3/9/16		Kit Inspection, Rifle, Smoke Helmet & Tower Respirator Inspection. Divine Service Y.50 Bty in action on Divisional Front.	
"	4/9/16		Route March, Squad Drill, Gun Drill 2" & 9.45", Rifle Exercise, Semaphore Telephony, Y.50 Bty in action on Divisional Front.	
"	5/9/16		Physical Drill, Gun Drill 2" & 9.45", Semaphore, Squad Drill, Rifle Exercise Telephony, Y.50 Bty in action on Divisional Front.	
"	6/9/16		Physical Drill, Squad Drill, Rifle Exercise, Semaphore, Telephony, Gun Drill 2" & 9.45". Building Gun Emplacements, Medium & Heavy. Y.50 Bty in action on Divisional Front.	
"	7/9/16		Route March. Gun Drill 2" & 9.45", Semaphore, Rifle Exercise, Telephony, Building Gun Emplacements, Medium & Heavy. Y.50 Bty in action on Divisional Front.	
"	8/9/16		Physical Drill. Firing Practice 2" & 9.45" Y.50 Bty in action on Divisional Front.	

T2131. Wt. W708–776. 500000. 4/15. Sir J. C. & S.

Army Form C. 2118.

Instructions regarding War Diaries and Intelligence Summaries are contained in F. S. Regs., Part II. and the Staff Manual respectively. Title pages will be prepared in manuscript.

WAR DIARY
or
INTELLIGENCE SUMMARY. of 50th DIVISIONAL TRENCH MORTAR BRIGADE

(Erase heading not required.)

SEPTEMBER 1916 VOLUME 3.

Place	Date	Hour	Summary of Events and Information	Remarks and references to Appendices
Sheet 57 D				
W26 c.34	1/9/16		Route March, Squad Drill, Rifle Exercise, Repairing Gun Positions, Semaphore. V.50 Bty carried out firing practice. Y.50 Bty in action on Divisional front.	
"	10/9/16		Kit Inspection, Rifle Smoke Helmet, Lower Respirator, ·303" Ammunition and Iron Rations Inspections. Divine Service. Y.50 relieved by 15th Div Trench Mortars. Handed over one 2" mortar in action on Divisional front. X.50 Bty proceeded into action and took over (1) Two 2" mortars from X.47th Div Trench Mortars in action. Z.50 Battery proceeded into action and took over (2) Two 2" mortars from 15th Div: Trench mortars in action. V.50 Bty fired 10 rounds 9.45" (practice)	
"	11/9/16		Physical Drill, Squad Parade, Rifle Exercise, Semaphore, Gun Drill. Y.50 Bty Inspection of Kits, Rifles, Respirators, checking of Bty Gun stores.	
	1[illegible]/9/16		Squad Drill, Gun Drill 2" & 9.45". Semaphore. V.50 [illegible] Y.50 [illegible] Batteries proceeded into action on Divisional Front. Left Rest Billets at about 5.30–6.0 pm.	
	1[illegible]/9/16		All Batteries in action on Divisional Front.	
	1[illegible]/9/16		ditto	
	15/9/16		ditto	

T.131. Wt. W708–776. 500,000. 4/15. Sir J. C. & S.

Instructions regarding War Diaries and Intelligence Summaries are contained in F. S. Regs., Part II. and the Staff Manual respectively. Title pages will be prepared in manuscript.

Army Form C. 2118.

WAR DIARY
or
INTELLIGENCE SUMMARY. of 50th Divisional Trench Mortar Brigade

(Erase heading not required.)

September 1916

Volume 3

Place	Date	Hour	Summary of Events and Information	Remarks and references to Appendices
Sheet 57D				
W.26 b.3.0	16/9/16		All Batteries in action on Divisional Front	
— " —	17/9/16		ditto	
— " —	18/9/16		ditto	
— " —	19/9/16		X.Y.Z. Batteries in action on Divisional Front. Part personnel V.50 Bty practice firing at Rest Billet.	
— " —	20/9/16		ditto.	
	21/9/16		ditto.	
— " —	22/9/16		X.Y.Z. Batteries in action on Divisional Front. V. Bty assisting Medium Btes.	
— " —	23/9/16		ditto.	
— " —	24/9/16		ditto.	
— " —	25/9/16		ditto	
— " —	26/9/16		ditto	
— " —	27/9/16		X.Y.Z. Btes in action on Divisional Front. V. Bty assisting Medium Btes. Vacated Billets at W26 b3.0. Sheet 57D at 9.30 am, arriving at new Billets (S.19.d 5 0) Sheet 57c at about 1. pm. Commenced erecting new camp.	

T2134. Wt. W708-776. 500000. 4/15. Sir J. C. & S.

Army Form C. 2118.

WAR DIARY
or
INTELLIGENCE SUMMARY. OF 50TH DIVISIONAL TRENCH MORTAR BRIGADE.
(Erase heading not required.)

Instructions regarding War Diaries and Intelligence Summaries are contained in F. S. Regs., Part II. and the Staff Manual respectively. Title pages will be prepared in manuscript.

SEPTEMBER 1916 VOLUME 3.

Place	Date	Hour	Summary of Events and Information	Remarks and references to Appendices
Sheet 57c S.19 d 6.0.	28/9/16		X.Y.Z Btes. in action on Divisional Front. Erecting new Camp, Physical	
—"—	29/9/16		ditto.	
—"—			Drill, Rifle Inspection, Semaphore, Squad Drill.	
—"—	30/9/16		X.Y.Z. Btes in action on Divisional Front. Building Erection of new Camp. Physical Drill.	

[signature] Captain R.A.
50th Divisional T.M. Officer

T2131. Wt. W708–776. 500,000. 4/15. Sir J. C. & S.

Army Form C. 2118.

Instructions regarding War Diaries and Intelligence Summaries are contained in F. S. Regs., Part II. and the Staff Manual respectively. Title pages will be prepared in manuscript.

WAR DIARY or INTELLIGENCE SUMMARY. of 50th DIVISIONAL TRENCH MORTAR BGDE.

(Erase heading not required.)

OCTOBER 1916. VOLUME 4 Vol 10

Place	Date	Hour	Summary of Events and Information	Remarks and references to Appendices
Sheet 57c.				
S.19.d.6.2.	1/10/16		X.Y.Z. Btes in action on Divisional Front. Kit inspection, Rifle and Respirator Inspection, for personnel in Billets.	
— " —	2/10/16		X.Y.Z. Btes in action on Divisional Front. Remainder of personnel performing fatigue duty in trenches.	
— " —	3/10/16		X.Y.Z. Btes in action on Divisional Front. Personnel in billets, fatigues.	
— " —	4/10/16		X.Y.Z. Btes relieved by 23rd Division. 2 officers, 21 other ranks proceeded to 4th Army trench mortar School for course of instruction in Medium and Heavy mortars.	
— " —	5/10/16		Fatigues; cleaning mortars, checking stores, etc; from trenches.	
— " —	6/10/16		Brigade Parade. Inspection of Clothing etc; Fatigues	
— " —	7/10/16		— " — Baths: Fatigues etc;	
— " —	8/10/16		Kit Inspection. '303 Ammunition, Iron Ration, & Smoke Helmet Inspections.	
— " —	9/10/16		Rifle Inspection. Gun Drill 9.45 inch. Fatigues.	
— " —	10/10/16		Fatigues: Gun Drill 2" & 9.45."	
— " —	11/10/16		— " —	
— " —	12/10/16		Semaphore, Rifle Drill. Physical Drill. Gun Drill.	

Instructions regarding War Diaries and Intelligence Summaries are contained in F. S. Regs., Part II. and the Staff Manual respectively. Title pages will be prepared in manuscript.

Army Form C. 2118.

WAR DIARY
or
INTELLIGENCE SUMMARY. of 50th DIVISIONAL TRENCH MORTAR BRIGADE.
(Erase heading not required.)

OCTOBER 1916. VOLUME 4.

Place	Date	Hour	Summary of Events and Information	Remarks and references to Appendices
Sheet 57c				
S.19.d.6.2.	13/10/16		Physical Drill, Squad Drill, Gun Drill 2" & 9.45". Rifle Exercises. Semaphore. Telephony.	
— " —	14/10/16		Route March. Rifle Exercise Fatigues	
— " —	15/10/16		Kit, Rifle, Smoke Helmet, Iron Ration and ·303 Ammunition Inspection.	
— " —	16/10/16		Physical Drill, Gun Drill, Rifle Exercise, Semaphore, Telephony, Squad Drill, Fatigues	
— " —	17/10/16		— " — — " — — " — — " —	
— " —	18/10/16		Constructing 2" and 9.45" Trench Mortar Emplacements.	
— " —	19/10/16		ditto. Physical Drill.	
— " —	20/10/16		Physical Drill. Gun Drill 2" & 9.45". Semaphore. Squad Drill. Rifle Exercise Telephony.	
— " —	21/10/16		Physical Drill. Gun Drill. 2" & 9.45" Semaphore. Squad Drill. Rifle Exercise. Telephony.	
— " —	22/10/16		Kit Inspection. Rifle Inspection. Smoke Helmet, Iron Ration & ·303 Ammunition Inspections.	
— " —	23/10/16		Physical Drill. Gun Drill 2" & 9.45". Semaphore. Rifle Exercise Squad Drill.	
— " —	24/10/16		Route March. Gun Drill 2" & 9.45".	
— " —	25/10/16		Physical Drill. Gun Drill 2" & 9.45". Rifle Drill. X.50 Medium Bty relieved 9th Division Trench Mortars in action on Divisional Front.	
— " —	26/10/16		Physical Drill. Gun Drill 2" & 9.45". Rifle Exercise Squad Drill Semaphore. X.50 Bty in action on Divisional Front.	

T2131. Wt. W708-776. 500,000. 4/15. Sir J. C. & S.

Instructions regarding War Diaries and Intelligence Summaries are contained in F. S. Regs., Part II. and the Staff Manual respectively. Title pages will be prepared in manuscript.

WAR DIARY
or
INTELLIGENCE SUMMARY. of 50th Divisional Trench Mortar Bgde.

(Erase heading not required.)

OCTOBER 1916

VOLUME 4

Army Form C. 2118.

Place	Date	Hour	Summary of Events and Information	Remarks and references to Appendices
Sheet 57c				
S.19.d.6.2.	27/10/16		Route March. Gun Drill 2" & 9.45". Semaphore, Squad Drill Rifle Drill. X.50 Bty in action on Divisional Front.	
— " —	28/10/16		Y.50 Bty relieved X.50 Bty in action on Divisional Front. Fatigues. 1 officer 32 other ranks, proceeded to 4th Army Trench Mortar School for course of instruction in 2" & 9.45" Mortars.	
— " —	29/10/16		Kit, Rifle, Smoke Helmet Iron Ration & ·303 Ammunition Inspections. Y.50 Battery in action on Divisional Front.	
— " —	30/10/16		Z.50 Bty proceeded into action on Divisional Front. Y.50 Battery in action on Divisional Front. Fatigues	
— " —	31/10/16		X.50 Battery relieved Y.50 Battery in action on Divisional Front. Fatigues	

R. MacDowell Lieut
a/50th Div'l T. M. Officer.

T2134. Wt. W708-776. 500000. 4/15. Sir J. C. & S.

Army Form C. 2118.

Instructions regarding War Diaries and Intelligence Summaries are contained in F. S. Regs., Part II. and the Staff Manual respectively. Title Pages will be prepared in manuscript.

WAR DIARY

~~INTELLIGENCE SUMMARY~~ of 50th Divisional Trench Mortar Brigade

(Erase heading not required.)

November 1916 Volume 5 Vol XI

Place	Date	Hour	Summary of Events and Information	Remarks and references to Appendices
Sheet 57c S.19.c.6.2.	1/11/16		X.50 Battery relieved Z.50 Battery in action on Divisional Front. Fatigues	
— " —	2/11/16		X.50 — " — in action on Divisional Front. Fatigues	
— " —	3/11/16		Y.50 — " — relieved X.50 Battery in action on Divisional Front. Fatigues.	
— " —	4/11/16		Fatigues. Y.50 Battery in action on Divisional Front. Z.50 Battery proceeded into action on Divisional Front.	
— " —	5/11/16		Z.50 Battery in action on Divisional Front. X.50 Battery relieved Y.50 Battery in action. Fatigues.	
— " —	6/11/16		Z.50 and X.50 Battery in action on Divisional Front. Inspection. Physical Drill, Rifle Drill, Semaphore, Gun Drill, Telephony.	
— " —	7/11/16		Z.50 and X.50 Battery (personnel only) withdrawn from the line, in accordance with instructions received from Div'l Headquarters. Guns left in situation. Gun Drill 2" 9.45" Rifle Drill Semaphore, Telephony	
— " —	8/11/16		Fatigues. Physical Drill.	
— " —	9/11/16		— " — — " — — " —	
— " —	10/11/16		— " — — " — — " —	
— " —	11/11/16		— " — — " — — " —	
— " —	12/11/16		Inspections: Kit, Rifle, Equipment & Ammunition.	

2449 Wt. W14957/M90 750,000 1/16 J.B.C. & A. Forms/C.2118/12.

Army Form C. 2118.

WAR DIARY

~~INTELLIGENCE SUMMARY~~

(Erase heading not required.)

Instructions regarding War Diaries and Intelligence Summaries are contained in F. S. Regs., Part II. and the Staff Manual respectively. Title Pages will be prepared in manuscript.

NOVEMBER. 1916 VOLUME 5. 50th DIVISIONAL TRENCH MORTAR BRIGADE.

Place	Date	Hour	Summary of Events and Information	Remarks and references to Appendices
Sheet 57c S.19 d 6.2.	13/11/16.		Fatigues. Telephony. Physical Drill.	
—"—	14/11/16		Fatigues. Physical Drill.	
—"—	15/11/16		Physical Drill. Gun Drill 2" and 9.45", Rifle Drill. Semaphore, Squad Drill. Fatigues. Telephony.	
—"—	16/11/16		Inspection. Physical Drill, Gun Drill 2" and 9.45." Rifle Drill. Semaphore Squad Drill. Telephony., Fatigues.	
—"—	17/11/16		Inspection: Physical Drill., Commenced withdrawing 2" mortars from line.	
—"—	18/11/16		Fatigues. completing withdrawal of 2" mortars from line.	
—"—	19/11/16		Inspection of Rifles, Kit (including leather equipment), Iron Rations, Smoke Helmets, ·303 ammunition. Fatigues. Relieved in line by 1st Division	
—"—	20/11/16		Inspection. Physical Drill. Telephony. Cleaning Gun Stores. Gun Drill Rifle Drill. Squad Drill.	
—"—	21/11/16		Squad Drill. Rifle Drill, Gun Drill.	
—"—	22/11/16		Telephony. ~~Gun~~ Drill, Rifle Exercise.	
—"—	23/11/16		Semaphore. Gun Drill. Squad Drill.	
—"—	24/11/16		Gun Drill. Telephony Squad Drill.	

Instructions regarding War Diaries and Intelligence Summaries are contained in F. S. Regs., Part II. and the Staff Manual respectively. Title Pages will be prepared in manuscript.

Army Form C. 2118.

WAR DIARY

or

~~INTELLIGENCE SUMMARY~~ OF 50TH DIVISIONAL TRENCH MORTAR BRIGADE

(Erase heading not required.)

NOVEMBER 1916. VOLUME 5

Place	Date	Hour	Summary of Events and Information	Remarks and references to Appendices
Sheet 51C S.19.d.6.2	25/11/16		Inspection (Bde). Gun Drill. Telephony. Rifle Drill.	
do.	26/11/16		do. do. Inspection of Rifles, Kit (including leather equipment) Iron Rations, Smoke Helmets, 303 Ammunition.	
do.	27/11/16		Route March (Bde). Gun Drill. Rifle Drill. Semaphore.	
do.	28/11/16		Gun Drill. Rifle Drill. Squad Drill. Telephony.	
do.	29/11/16		Fatigues. Field Service Marching Order Inspection.	
do.	30/11/16		do. do. do. Squad Drill.	

M. A. Macnamara. Capt. R.F.A.
O/50th Div'l Trench Mortar Officer.

2449 Wt. W14957/M90 750,000 1/16 J.B.C. & A. Forms/C.2118/12.

Army Form C. 2118.

WAR DIARY
or
INTELLIGENCE SUMMARY OF 50TH DIVISIONAL TRENCH MORTAR BRIGADE.

(Erase heading not required.)

Instructions regarding War Diaries and Intelligence Summaries are contained in F. S. Regs., Part II. and the Staff Manual respectively. Title Pages will be prepared in manuscript.

DECEMBER, 1916. VOLUME No: 6

Vol 12

Place	Date	Hour	Summary of Events and Information	Remarks and references to Appendices
Sheet 62D C.13.c.3.7.	1/12/16.		The Brigade less 1 officer and 20 Other Ranks proceeded to rest area at BEHENCOURT. arriving at 1·30pm.	
— " —	2/12/16.		Inspection of Rifles, Kit. Fatigues.	
— " —	3/12/16		Inspection; (Brigade) Physical Drill. Church Parade	
— " —	4/12/16		Full Marching Order. (Route March).	
— " —	5/12/16		—— do ——	
— " —	6/12/16		Rifle Drill, Physical Drill; Fatigues.	
— " —	7/12/16		Brigade Parade Full Marching Order: (Route March)	
— " —	8/12/16		Rifle Drill. Physical Drill. Fatigues. X. Bty proceeded to camp (S.19.d.5.0) to relieve personnel of V. Bty	
— " —	9/12/16		Rifle Drill. Physical Exercise Ceremonial Drill. Fatigues.	
— " —	10/12/16		Inspection (Bde). Physical Drill. Church Parade.	
— " —	11/12/16		Route March. Baths. Fatigues.	
— " —	12/12/16		Inspection, Full Marching Order. Route March, Rifle Drill. Fatigues.	
— " —	13/12/16		—— do. ——	
B.12.c.4.8. Sheet 62D.	14/12/16		V.50 Battery proceeded to 4th Army School of Mortars at VAUX EN AMIENOIS. The remainder of the Brigade, vacated billets at BEHENCOURT and proceeded to BEAUCOURT.	

2449 Wt. W14957/M90 750,000 1/16 J.B.C. & A. Forms/C.2118/12.

Army Form C. 2118.

Instructions regarding War Diaries and Intelligence Summaries are contained in F. S. Regs., Part II. and the Staff Manual respectively. Title Pages will be prepared in manuscript.

WAR DIARY
or
INTELLIGENCE SUMMARY of 50th Divisional Trench Mortar Brigade.

(Erase heading not required.)

December 1916. Volume No:- 6

Place	Date	Hour	Summary of Events and Information	Remarks and references to Appendices
Sheet 62 d [illegible] B.12 C 4.9.	15/12/16		Z.50 Battery relieved X.50 Battery in camp at Forward Area (319 d 5.0) Gun Drill. Route March.	
"	16/12/16		Parade:- Full Marching Order. 25 Other Ranks attached to 50th D.A.C. for duty. Gun Drill.	
"	17/12/16		Fatigues.	
"	18/12/16		Fatigues. Gun Drill 2".	
"	19/12/16		Fatigues. 2" Trench Mortar Demonstration, at 3rd Corps School MONTIGNY. Fired 15 rounds.	
"	20/12/16		Kit Inspection. Gun Drill. Semaphore, Rifle Drill.	
"	21/12/16		Full Marching Order Parade. Route March. Fatigues.	
"	22/12/16		Brigade Inspection. Rifle Drill & Exercises. Fatigues.	
"	23/12/16		ditto. 25 Other ranks rejoined from 50th D.A.C.	
"	24/12/16		Kit Inspection. Physical Drill. Fatigues. Y.50 Battery returned from 4th Army Trench Mortar School.	
"	25/12/16		Inspection, Divine Service. Holy Communion.	
"	26/12/16		Brigade Inspection. Rifle Inspection. Physical Drill. Smoke Helmet Drill.	
"	27/12/16		Brigade Inspection. Route March.	
"	28/12/16		Inspection of Shrapnel Helmets. Physical Drill. Signalling. Gun Drill. Rifle Drill.	

2449 Wt. W14957/M90 750,000 1/16 J.B.C. & A. Forms/C.2118/12.

Army Form C. 2118.

WAR DIARY
or
INTELLIGENCE SUMMARY OF 50th DIVISIONAL TRENCH MORTAR BRIGADE.

Instructions regarding War Diaries and Intelligence Summaries are contained in F. S. Regs., Part II. and the Staff Manual respectively. Title Pages will be prepared in manuscript.

(Erase heading not required.)

DECEMBER 1916. VOLUME No:- 6

Place	Date	Hour	Summary of Events and Information	Remarks and references to Appendices
Sheet 62D B12 C 4-8	29/12/16		Proceeded to Forward Area S-19.d-50. Left BEAUCOURT at 8-30 a.m. Arrived at Forward Area at 12 noon. Fatigues. Party of 25 N.C.O's and men proceeded to 50th D.A.C for duty.	
Sheet 57D. S.19 d 5.0.	30/12/16		Brigade Inspection. Telephony Fatigues.	
— " —	31/12/16		Brigade Inspection. Fatigues. Officers and N.C.O's proceeded to trenches to locate positions etc for 2 inch and 9.45 inch Trench Mortars.	

H. C. Macnamara. Capt R.F.A.
50th Divisional Trench Mortar Officer.

2449 Wt. W14957/M90 750,000 1/16 J.B.C. & A. Forms/C.2118/12.

Instructions regarding War Diaries and Intelligence Summaries are contained in F. S. Regs., Part II. and the Staff Manual respectively. Title Pages will be prepared in manuscript.

Army Form C. 2118.

WAR DIARY
or
INTELLIGENCE SUMMARY of 50th DIVISIONAL TRENCH MORTAR BRIGADE.

(Erase heading not required.)

JANUARY 1917. VOLUME No: X

Place	Date	Hour	Summary of Events and Information	Remarks and references to Appendices
Sheet 57D S19 d.50.	1/1/17		Brigade Inspection. X.50 Battery proceeded into action to relieve X.1 Battery 1st Division. Fatigues.	
—	2/1/17		X.50 Battery in action on Divisional Front. Inspection. Physical Drill. Telephony. Fatigues.	
—	3/1/17		——— ditto ——— Brigade Inspection. V.50 Heavy Battery proceeded to trenches to work on emplacement for 9.45" Mortar. [illegible]. Fatigues.	
—	4/1/17		Y.50 Battery relieved X.50 Battery in action on Divisional Front. V.50 Heavy Battery continued work on emplacement, assisted by Z.50 Battery. Fatigues.	
—	5/1/17		Y.50 Battery in action on Divisional Front. V.50 Battery working on Emplacement. Fatigue Party attached to D.A.C. for duty rejoined.	
—	6/1/17		Y.50 Battery in action on Divisional Front. V.50 Battery working on [illegible]. Telephony. Fatigues. Fifteen Reinforcements arrived.	
—	7/1/17		Z.50 Battery relieved Y.50 Battery in action on Divisional Front. V.50 Battery working on emplacement. Telephone classes. Fatigues.	
—	8/1/17		Z.50 Battery in action on Divisional Front. V.50 Battery working on emplacement. Fatigues.	
—	9/1/17		Z.50 Battery in action on Divisional Front. V.50 Battery completed emplacement. X.50 Battery conveyed 9.45" Mortar to Emplacement and 25 rounds ammunition. [illegible] position ready for action.	
—	10/1/17		Y.50 Battery relieved Z.50 Battery in action on Divisional Front. V.50 Battery proceeded to gun position leaving camp at 5 pm. Fatigues.	

2449 Wt. W14957/M90 750,000 1/16 J.B.C. & A. Forms/C.2118/12.

Army Form C. 2118.

Instructions regarding War Diaries and Intelligence Summaries are contained in F. S. Regs., Part II. and the Staff Manual respectively. Title Pages will be prepared in manuscript.

WAR DIARY
or
INTELLIGENCE SUMMARY of 50th DIVISIONAL TRENCH MORTAR BRIGADE.
(Erase heading not required.)

JANUARY 1917

VOLUME No: 7

Place	Date	Hour	Summary of Events and Information	Remarks and references to Appendices
Sheet 57d. S17d.50	11/1/17		Y.50 Battery in action on Divisional Front. V.50 Battery in action on Divisional Front. Fired 24 rounds 9.45". Very good results. Revolver Drill Classes. Fatigues.	
— " —	12/1/17		Y.50 Battery in action on Divisional Front. Inspection of small arms and instruction in their use. Fatigues.	
— " —	13/1/17		X.50 Battery relieved Y.50 Battery in action on Divisional Front. Telephone Classes. Fatigues. Commenced working on two new 2" emplacements.	
— " —	14/1/17		X.50 Battery in action on Divisional Front. Kit Inspection. Fatigues. Work on 2" Emplacements.	
— " —	15/1/17		X.50 Battery in action on Divisional Front. Working on 2" Emplacements. One emplacement completed ready for firing. V.50 Battery working on emplacement for 9.45" Mortar. Physical Drill. Rifle Drill Gun Drill. Fatigues.	
— " —	16/1/17		Z.50 Battery relieved X.50 Battery in action on Divisional Front. Working on 2" Emplacement. V.50 Battery continuing work on emplacement. Telephone Classes. Fatigues.	
— " —	17/1/17		Z.50 Battery in action on Divisional Front. Working on 2" Emplacements. V.50 Battery continuing work on Emplacement. Fatigues.	
— " —	18/1/17		Z.50 Battery in action on Divisional Front. Working on 2" Emplacements. V.50 Battery continuing work on Emplacement. Fatigues.	

2449 Wt. W14957/M90 750,000 1/16 J.B.C. & A. Forms/C.2118/12.

Army Form C. 2118.

Instructions regarding War Diaries and Intelligence Summaries are contained in F. S. Regs., Part II. and the Staff Manual respectively. Title Pages will be prepared in manuscript.

WAR DIARY
or
INTELLIGENCE SUMMARY of 50th Divisional Trench Mortar Brigade

(Erase heading not required.)

JANUARY 1917. Volume No. 7.

Place	Date	Hour	Summary of Events and Information	Remarks and references to Appendices
Sheet 57a. S.19.d.50.	19/1/17		X.50 Battery relieved Z.50 Battery in action on Divisional Front. Fatigues. V.50 Battery working on Emplacement.	
"	20/1/17		X.50 Battery in action on Divisional Front. Fired two rounds. Inspection. Telephone Classes. Fatigues.	
"	21/1/17		X.50 Battery in action on Divisional Front. Kit Inspection. Fatigues.	
"	22/1/17		Y.50 Battery relieved X.50 Battery in action on Divisional Front. Inspection. Telephone Classes. Rifle Drill. Fatigues	
"	23/1/17		Y.50 Battery in action on Divisional Front. Fatigues.	
"	23/1/17		Y.50 Battery in action on Divisional Front. Route March. Fatigues.	
"	24/1/17		Z.50 Battery relieved Y.50 Battery in action on Divisional Front. Inspection.	
"	25/1/17		Foot Marching Order. Fatigues. Gun Drill 2".	
"	26/1/17		Z.50 Battery in action on Divisional Front. Brigade Inspection. Route March. Fatigues. Z.50 Battery fired two rounds 2".	
"	27/1/17		Z.50 Battery in action on Divisional Front. Inspection. Route March (Marching Order).	
"	28/1/17		Brigade relieved in action on Divisional Front by 1st Australian Division. Fatigues.	
"	29/1/17		Brigade vacated camp at S.19 d.50 and proceeded to billets at MOLLIENS-AU-BOIS. Left camp at 8.0 am. Move completed by 6.pm.	

2449 Wt. W14957/M90 750,000 1/16 J.B.C. & A. Forms/C.2118/12.

Army Form C. 2118.

Instructions regarding War Diaries and Intelligence Summaries are contained in F. S. Regs., Part II. and the Staff Manual respectively. Title Pages will be prepared in manuscript.

WAR DIARY
or
INTELLIGENCE SUMMARY of 50th Divisional Trench Mortar Brigade.

(Erase heading not required.)

January 1917 — Volume No: 7

Place	Date	Hour	Summary of Events and Information	Remarks and references to Appendices
B.7.b.3.5	30/1/17		Fatigues.	
— . —	31/1/17		Brigade Inspection. Route March. Fatigues.	

[illegible signature] Capt R.F.A.
50th Div'l T. M. officer

2449 Wt. W14957/M90 750,000 1/16 J.B.C. & A. Forms/C.2118/12.

Army Form C. 2118.

WAR DIARY
or
INTELLIGENCE SUMMARY
of 5th Divisional Trench Mortar Brigade.

(*Erase heading not required.*)

Instructions regarding War Diaries and Intelligence Summaries are contained in F. S. Regs., Part II. and the Staff Manual respectively. Title Pages will be prepared in manuscript.

February 1917 — Volume No 8. — Page 1.

Place	Date	Hour	Summary of Events and Information	Remarks and references to Appendices
B.7 b.3.5	1/2/17		Brigade Inspection. Inspection of all materiel on charge. Physical Drill. Fatigues.	
— " —	2/2/17		Brigade Inspection. Route March. Rifle Drill. Fatigues.	
— " —	3/2/17		Brigade Inspection. Rifle Drill. Foot Drill. Fatigues.	
— " —	4/2/17		Brigade Inspection (Marching Order) Route March. Fatigues.	
— " —	5.2.17		The Brigade vacated billets at MOLLIENS-AU-BOIS at 9.0 a.m. and proceeded to billets at HAMELET arriving there at 1.30pm. Fatigues	
HAMELET	6/2/17		Brigade Inspection. Marching Order less packs. Route March. Gun Drill. Foot Drill.	
— " —	7/2/17		Brigade Inspection. Foot Drill. Route March. Fatigues.	
— " —	8/2/17		Brigade Inspection. Marching Order; Route March.	
— " —	9/2/17		Brigade Inspection Marching Order. Route March.	
— " —	10/2/17		Brigade Inspection. Route March. N.C.O's. Lecture. subject "DISCIPLINE"	
— " —	11/2/17		Brigade Inspection Route March. Fatigues.	
— " —	12/2/17		Brigade Inspection. Route March. Full Marching Order. Advance Party proceeded to Forward Area. Fatigues.	
— " —	13/2/17		The Brigade vacated billets at HAMELET, at 8.45 a.m. and proceeded to Forward Area M.27 a 7.5, Sheet 62 C S.W. Arriving there at 1.30 pm. V.50 Battery proceeded to trenches preparing emplacements. Fatigues.	
M.27 a 7.5	14/2/17		X and Y Batteries proceeded to trenches to prepare emplacements. V Battery continuing work on emplacement. Fatigues.	

2449 Wt. W14957/M90 750,000 1/16 J.B.C. & A. Forms/C.2118/12.

Army Form C. 2118.

Instructions regarding War Diaries and Intelligence Summaries are contained in F. S. Regs., Part II. and the Staff Manual respectively. Title Pages will be prepared in manuscript.

WAR DIARY
or
~~INTELLIGENCE SUMMARY~~ of 50th Divisional Trench Mortar Brigade.

(Erase heading not required.)

FEBRUARY 1917. VOLUME No: 8. PAGE II

Place	Date	Hour	Summary of Events and Information	Remarks and references to Appendices
Sheet 62c SW M.27.d.75	15/2/17		V.X.+Y. Batterys continuing work on emplacements. Fatigues.	
— " —	16/2/17		ditto.	
— " —	17/2/17		ditto.	
— " —	18/2/17		ditto.	
— " —	19/2/17		Z.50 Battery relieved Y.50 Battery in trenches. V.X and Z. Batterys continued work on emplacements. Fatigues.	
— " —	20/2/17		V.X and Z. Batterys continued work on emplacements. Y.50 Battery detached for duty with 48th Division.	
— " —	21/2/17		V.X and Z. Batterys continued work on emplacements. Fatigues	
— " —	22/2/17		ditto.	
— " —	23/2/17		V.X and Z Batterys continued work on emplacements. Half X.50 Battery detached for duty with 48th Division.	
— " —	24/2/17		V.X and Z. Battery's continued work on emplacements. ditto. X.50 Battery fired 8 rounds	
— " —	25/2/17		2". Very good results. V.X and Z. Battery's continued work on emplacements.	
— " —	26/2/17		ditto.	
— " —	27/2/17		ditto.	
— " —	28/2/17			

M.C. Macnamara. Capt R.F.A.
50th Div'l T. M. Officer.

2449 Wt. W14957/M90 750,000 1/16 J.B.C. & A. Forms/C.2118/12.

CONFIDENTIAL.

B.M./M.

Headquarters,

50th Division.

In continuation of my B.M./M dated 1.4.17.

Herewith War Diary for 50th Divisional Trench Mortars for the month of March 1917.

Lieut-Col.,
A/C.R.A. 50th Division.

2. 4. 17.

Army Form C. 2118.

WAR DIARY
or
INTELLIGENCE SUMMARY OF 50TH DIVISIONAL TRENCH MORTAR BRIGADE
(Erase heading not required.)

Instructions regarding War Diaries and Intelligence Summaries are contained in F. S. Regs., Part II. and the Staff Manual respectively. Title Pages will be prepared in manuscript.

MARCH 1917. VOLUME No: 9 Vol 15

Place	Date	Hour	Summary of Events and Information	Remarks and references to Appendices
SHEET 62C SW M.27.d.7.5	1/3/17.		V. X. and Z. Battery's continuing work on emplacements. Fatigues.	
— " —	2/3/17		ditto.	
— " —	3/3/17		ditto.	
— " —	4/3/17		ditto. X.50 Battery fired 20 rounds 2". Z.50 Battery fired 15 rounds. 2".	
— " —	5/3/17		X. and Z. Battery's continuing work on emplacements. Personnel of V. Battery less 5. O.R's returned to Billets, on completion of emplacement for 9.45" Mortar	
— " —	6/3/17		X & Z. Battery's continuing work on emplacements. Fatigues. Y.50 Battery and half X.50 Battery rejoined from attachment to 48th Division	
— " —	7/3/17		X & Z Battery's continuing work on emplacements. Fatigues.	
— " —	8/3/17		ditto.	
— " —	9/3/17		Y.50 Battery relieved Z.50 Battery in trenches. X & Y. Battery's working on emplacements, and repairing bomb stores. Fatigues.	
— " —	10/3/17		X & Y. Battery's working on emplacements. Brigade Inspection. Fatigues.	
— " —	11/3/17		X & Y. Battery's working on emplacements. Brigade Inspection. Rifle drill. Fatigues.	
— " —	12/3/17		ditto.	
— " —	13/3/17		X & Y. Batterys working on emplacements. Brigade Inspection. Rifle drill Physical drill.	

2449 Wt. W14957/M90 750,000 1/16 J.B.C. & A. Forms/C.2118/12.

Instructions regarding War Diaries and Intelligence Summaries are contained in F. S. Regs., Part II. and the Staff Manual respectively. Title Pages will be prepared in manuscript.

Army Form C. 2118.

WAR DIARY
or
INTELLIGENCE SUMMARY OF 50TH DIVISIONAL TRENCH MORTAR BRIGADE.

(Erase heading not required.)

March 1917 Volume No. 9

Place	Date	Hour	Summary of Events and Information	Remarks and references to Appendices
M.27.d.7.5.	14/3/17		X & Y Battery's working on emplacements. V.50 Battery personnel proceeded to trenches to work on emplacements. Brigade Inspection. Rifle Drill. Physical Drill. Fatigues.	
— " —	15/3/17		ditto.	
— " —	16/3/17		X Y & V Battery's working on emplacements. Fatigues. Half Z.50 Battery proceeded to trenches to relieve half X.50 Battery. Fatigues.	
— " —	17/3/17		X.50 Battery fired 15 rounds 2". Y.50 Battery fired 60 rounds 2". V.50 Battery fired 17 rounds 9.45". Very good results. Z.50 Battery relieved Y.50 Battery in trenches. Fatigues.	
— " —	18/3/17		X Z & V. Battery's cleaning guns, stores, bombs, etc; Fatigues	
— " —	19/3/17		Personnel in rest billets proceeded to line, to assist X.Z. & V Battery's to clear positions etc.	
— " —	20/3/17		ditto.	
— " —	21/3/17		Guns withdrawn from positions. Full Marching Order Inspection. Gun Drill. 2". Instructing part personnel of 59th Division T.M.B. in Trench Mortars. Preparing stores, etc, for handing over.	
— " —	22/3/17		The Brigade vacated billets at M.27.d.7.5. at 1.30pm and arrived at HAMELET at 3.30pm. Fatigues. Handed over all Corps and Area Stores. All 2" and 9.45" Ammunition and One 9.45" Trench Mortar.	
HAMELET	23/3/17		Kit, Small Arm, and Leather Equipment Inspections. Fatigues.	
— " —	24/3/17		Bde Inspection in Full Marching Order (less packs). Instructions in Use of Small Box Respirator, Musketry, Physical Drill,	

2449 Wt. W14957/M90 750,000 1/16 J.B.C. & A. Forms/C.2118/12.

Army Form C. 2118.

Instructions regarding War Diaries and Intelligence Summaries are contained in F. S. Regs., Part II. and the Staff Manual respectively. Title Pages will be prepared in manuscript.

WAR DIARY
or
INTELLIGENCE SUMMARY of 50th DIVISIONAL TRENCH MORTAR BRIGADE

(Erase heading not required.)

MARCH 1917 VOLUME No: 9.

Place	Date	Hour	Summary of Events and Information	Remarks and references to Appendices
HAMELET	25.3.17		Brigade Inspection. Route March. Instruction in use of Small Box Respirator. Fatigues.	
— " —	26/3/17		Brigade Inspection. General Fatigues.	
— " —	27/3/17		ditto.	
OCCOCHES.	28/3/17		The Brigade vacated billets at HAMELET at 7-0am and proceeded to OCCOCHES arriving at 3.30pm Fatigues.	
— " —	29/3/17		Fatigues.	
— " —	30/3/17		Fatigues. Rifle and Revolver Inspection. Revolver practice shooting on miniature range.	
— " —	31/3/17		Instruction in use of Small Box Respirator. Rifle practice shooting on miniature range. Fatigues.	

W. C. Stead Capt R.A.
O.C. 50th Div'l Trench Mortar Brigade

2449 Wt. W14957/M90 750,000 1/16 J.B.C. & A. Forms/C.2118/12.

Army Form C. 2118.

Instructions regarding War Diaries and Intelligence Summaries are contained in F. S. Regs., Part II. and the Staff Manual respectively. Title Pages will be prepared in manuscript.

WAR DIARY
or
INTELLIGENCE SUMMARY of 50th Divisional Trench Mortar Brigade

(Erase heading not required.)

April 1917 — Volume No. 10 — Part I

Place	Date	Hour	Summary of Events and Information	Remarks and references to Appendices
OCCOCHES.	1/4/17		Brigade Inspection. Kit Inspection. Rifle Inspection. Fatigues.	
— " —	2/4/17		Brigade Inspection. Fatigues. Rifle Drill. Semaphore.	
— " —	3/4/17		Brigade Inspection. Fatigues. X & Z. Battery's proceeded by march route to BEAUMETZ leaving Headquarters at 1·0 p.m.	
— " —	4/4/17		The remainder of the Brigade vacated billets at OCCOCHES at 6·0 a.m. and proceeded to WAILLY. arriving at 3·30 p.m., together with X & Z Battery's. Erecting Bell Tents & Shelters.	
WAILLY	5/4/17		Brigade Inspection. 4 officers and 84 O.R's. detached for duty with Divisional Artillery	
			Fatigues	
— " —	6/4/17		Fatigues.	
— " —	7/4/17		Fatigues.	
— " —	8/4/17		Fatigues.	
— " —	9/4/17		Rifle, and Gas Helmet Inspections. Fatigues.	
— " —	10/4/17		Fatigues.	
— " —	11/4/17		Fatigues.	
— " —	12/4/17		Fatigues.	
— " —	13/4/17		Fatigues. Party rejoined from attached 50th Divisional Artillery.	
— " —	14/4/17		Brigade Inspection. Fatigues.	
— " —	15/4/17		Fatigues.	
— " —	16/4/17		The Brigade vacated billets at WAILLY at 9·30 am and proceeded to ARRAS arriving at 11·20 a.m. Fatigues.	

Army Form C. 2118.

Instructions regarding War Diaries and Intelligence Summaries are contained in F. S. Regs., Part II. and the Staff Manual respectively. Title Pages will be prepared in manuscript.

WAR DIARY
or
INTELLIGENCE SUMMARY of 50th Divisional Trench Mortar Brigade

(Erase heading not required.)

April 1917 VOLUME No: 10 PAGE II

Place	Date	Hour	Summary of Events and Information	Remarks and references to Appendices
ARRAS	17/4/17		Inspection of all Gun Stores on charge. Fatigues. Cleaning Guns, Gun Stores, Etc;	
-"-	18/4/17		Fatigues.	
-"-	19/4/17		Fatigues.	
-"-	20/4/17		Fatigues.	
	21/4/17		Fatigues.	
-"-	22/4/17		Fatigues.	
-"-	23/4/17		Fatigues.	
-"-	24/4/17		Fatigues.	
-"-	25/4/17		Fatigues.	
-"-	26/4/17		Kit Inspection. Rifle, Revolver and Ammunition Inspection. Equipment, Box Respirator and P.H. Helmet Inspection. Mess Tin Inspection.	
-"-	27/4/17		Route March. Skeleton Marching Order. Fatigues.	
-"-	28/4/17		Gun Drill 2" Route March. Rifle Drill. Fatigues.	
-"-	29/4/17		Brigade Inspection. Kit Inspection.	
-"-	30/4/17		Party of 4 officers, 54 O.R's proceeded to III Army Trench Mortar School on course of instruction. Fatigues.	

[signature]
Capt R.F.A.
O.C. 50th Div T. M. Bde.

Instructions regarding War Diaries and Intelligence Summaries are contained in F. S. Regs., Part II. and the Staff Manual respectively. Title Pages will be prepared in manuscript.

Army Form C. 2118.

WAR DIARY
or
INTELLIGENCE SUMMARY of 50th Divisional Trench Mortar ~~Brigade~~ Batteries

(Erase heading not required.)

MAY. 1917 — Volume No. 11 — Vol 17

Place	Date	Hour	Summary of Events and Information	Remarks and references to Appendices
ARRAS.	1/5/17		Gun Drill. 2" T.M. Guard Mounting & Rifle Drill. Fatigues.	
— " —	2/5/17		Gun Drill 2" T.M. Guard Mounting & Rifle Drill. Fatigues.	
— " —	3/5/17		Gun Drill. 2" T.M. Guard Mounting & Rifle Drill. Fatigues.	
— " —	4/5/17		Inspection of Smoke Helmets, Field Dressings, Iron Rations & Identity Discs. Full Marching Order Inspection. Fatigues.	
— " —	5/5/17		Route March.	
— " —	6/5/17		Brigade Inspection. Full Marching Order. Inspection of Clothing, Small Kit, etc.	
— " —	7/5/17		Route March. Gun Drill. Rifle Drill. Fatigues.	
— " —	8/5/17		Brigade Parade. Guard Mounting Drill. Rifle Drill. Gun Drill. 4 Officers & 54 Other Ranks rejoined from III Army Trench M. School on completion of course of instruction.	
— " —	9/5/17		Semaphore. Fatigues.	
— " —	10/5/17		Route March. 36 Other Ranks proceeded to III Army T. M. School for course of instruction in Trench Mortars.	
— " —	11/5/17		Brigade Parade, Semaphore, Rifle Drill. Guard Mounting. Mess Tin Inspection. Fatigues.	
— " —	12/5/17		Brigade Inspection. Route March. Fatigues.	
— " —	13/5/17		Kit Inspection. Rifle Inspection. Gas Helmet Inspection.	
— " —	14/5/17		Brigade Inspection. Full Marching Order. Route March. Skeleton Order.	
— " —	15/5/17		Brigade Parade. Full Marching Order. Fatigues.	

2449 Wt. W14957/M90 750,000 1/16 J.B.C. & A. Forms/C.2118/12.

Army Form C. 2118.

Instructions regarding War Diaries and Intelligence Summaries are contained in F. S. Regs., Part II. and the Staff Manual respectively. Title Pages will be prepared in manuscript.

WAR DIARY or INTELLIGENCE SUMMARY OF 50th DIVISIONAL TRENCH MORTAR BATTERIES.

(Erase heading not required.)

MAY 1917. VOLUME No: 11

Place	Date	Hour	Summary of Events and Information	Remarks and references to Appendices
ARRAS	16/5/17		Squad Drill. Semaphore. Rifle Drill. Fatigues.	
—"—	17/5/17		Route March. Fatigues.	
—"—	18/5/17		Rifle Drill, Semaphore & Telephony. Squad Drill.	
—"—	19/5/17		Physical Drill. Semaphore. Rifle Drill. Fatigues. 36 O.R's rejoined from III Army T.M. School.	
—"—	20/5/17		Inspection: Full Marching Order. Rifle, Kit, Equipment & Box Respirator Inspections.	
—"—	21/5/17		Route March. Skeleton Order. Refitting of Box Respirators.	
—"—	22/5/17		Fatigues. Inspection of Iron Rations.	
—"—	23/5/17		Squad Drill, Semaphore. Guard Mounting & Rifle Drill. Fatigues.	
—"—	24/5/17		Medium and Heavy Batteries proceeded by march route to MONCHIET, leaving ARRAS about 9.30am and arriving at MONCHIET about 1 pm. Fatigues.	
MONCHIET	25/5/17		Route March. Semaphore. Rifle Drill.	
MONCHIET	26/5/17		Medical Examination Rifle Drill, Squad Drill. Semaphore.	
—"—	27/5/17		Inspection Full Marching Order. Church Parade. Fatigues.	
—"—	28/5/17		Route March. Rifle Drill. Guard Mounting. Fatigues.	
—"—	29/5/17		Fitting of Equipment. Fatigues. Medical Inspection. 2" Gun Drill.	
—"—	30/5/17		Rifle Drill. Squad Drill. Semaphore 2" Gun Drill. Fatigues.	
—"—	31/5/17		Squad Drill. Semaphore. 2" Gun Drill. Fatigues.	

[signature] Capt. R.F.A.
Comdg 50th Div T. M. Batteries

2449 Wt. W14957/M90 750,000 1/16 J.B.C. & A. Forms/C.2118/12.

Army Form C. 2118.

Instructions regarding War Diaries and Intelligence Summaries are contained in F. S. Regs., Part II. and the Staff Manual respectively. Title Pages will be prepared in manuscript.

WAR DIARY
or
INTELLIGENCE SUMMARY of 50th Divisional Trench Mortar Batteries

(Erase heading not required.)

June 1917. VOLUME No 12

Place	Date	Hour	Summary of Events and Information	Remarks and references to Appendices
MONCHIET	1/6/17		Reinforcements Gun Drill. Fatigues.	
—,,—	2/6/17		Rifle Drill. Gun Drill. Squad Drill, Semaphore. Reinforcements Gun Drill Fatigues.	
—,,—	3/6/17		Church Parades. Fatigues.	
—,,—	4/6/17		Squad Drill. Semaphore. Rifle Drill. Reinforcements Gun Drill. Fatigues.	
—,,—	5/6/17		——— do. ———	Medical Inspection.
—,,—	6/6/17		——— do. ———	
—,,—	7/6/17		Rifle Drill. Squad Drill. Fatigues.	
—,,—	8/6/17		Fatigues.	
—,,—	9/6/17		—,,—. Party of 2 officers and 40 Other Ranks detached for duty with Divisional Artillery.	
—,,—	10/6/17		Kit, Rifle, Revolver, Iron Ration, and ·303 Ammunition Inspections. Full Marching Order Inspection. Fatigues.	
—,,—	11/6/17		Squad Drill, Rifle Drill, Reinforcements Gun Drill, Semaphore. Fatigues.	
—,,—	12/6/17		——— do. ———	Medical Inspection.
—,,—	13/6/17		——— do ———	
—,,—	14/6/17		Route March. Fatigues.	
—,,—	15/6/17		Route March. A Practice 2" T. M. Shoot was carried out, 8 rounds were fired.	
—,,—	16/6/17		Reinforcements Gun Drill, Fatigues.	
—,,—	17/6/17		Medium & Heavy T. M. Batteries vacated camp at MONCHIET at 8·0 a.m. and proceeded to BOIRY-BECQUERELLE arriving about 10·15 a.m. Fatigues.	

2449 Wt. W14957/M90 750,000 1/16 J.B.C. & A. Forms/C.2118/12.

Army Form C. 2118.

Instructions regarding War Diaries and Intelligence Summaries are contained in F. S. Regs., Part II. and the Staff Manual respectively. Title Pages will be prepared in manuscript.

WAR DIARY
or
~~INTELLIGENCE~~ SUMMARY OF 50TH DIVISIONAL TRENCH MORTAR BATTERIES

(Erase heading not required.)

JUNE 1917 VOLUME No:12

Place	Date	Hour	Summary of Events and Information	Remarks and references to Appendices
BOIRY BECQUERELLE	18/6/17		Fatigues	
— " —	19/6/17		Full Marching Order Parade. The 4 Battery's less Hd Qrs proceeded to a Forward Camp at HENIN (N 32 d 7.3 Sheet 51B) Fatigues. Preparing 9.45" T. M. Emplacements.	
— " —	20/6/17		Fatigues. Preparing 9.45" T. M. Emplacements	
— " —	21/6/17		do	
— " —	22/6/17		do	
— " —	23/6/17		do	
— " —	24/6/17		do.	
— " —	25/6/17		do.	
— " —	26/6/17		do. O's. C. Y. & Z Battery's reconnoitred positions for 2" Mortars.	
— " —	27/6/17		Fatigues. Preparing 9.45" and 2" T. M. Emplacements.	
— " —	28/6/17		do	
— " —	29/6/17		do.	
— " —	30/6/17		do.	

S. R. C. Phinn[?] Capt R.F.A.
50th Div'l Trench M. Officer.

2449 Wt. W14957/M90 750,000 1/16 J.B.C. & A. Forms/C.2118/12.

Army Form C. 2118.

Instructions regarding War Diaries and Intelligence Summaries are contained in F. S. Regs., Part II. and the Staff Manual respectively. Title Pages will be prepared in manuscript.

WAR DIARY
or
INTELLIGENCE SUMMARY of 50th DIVISIONAL TRENCH MORTAR BATTERIES.

(Erase heading not required.)

JULY 1917 VOLUME No: 13

Place	Date	Hour	Summary of Events and Information	Remarks and references to Appendices
BOIRY BECQUERELLE	1/7/17		Fatigues. Preparing 9.45" & 2" T. M. Emplacements.	
— " —	2/7/17		——— do ———	
— " —	3/7/17		——— do ———	
— " —	4/7/17		——— do ———	
— " —	5/7/17		——— do ———	
— " —	6/7/17		——— do ———	
— " —	7/7/17		——— do. ———	
— " —	8/7/17		Fatigues. Emplacements for 9.45" and 2" T. M.'s completed.	
— " —	9/7/17		Fatigues. A bombardment of FONTAINE TRENCH and NARROW TRENCH and points in rear was carried out from 4.0pm till 5.15 pm. 110 rounds 2" and 41 rounds 9.45" were fired. A number of direct hits were observed and timber and other material were thrown up.	
— " —	10/7/17		Fatigues. V. X. Z. Batteries in action on Divisional Front.	
— " —	11.7.17		— " —. ——— do ———	
— " —	12.7.17		— " —. ——— do ———	
— " —	13.7.17		— " —. Fired 10 rounds 2". Very good results. Inspection of Anti-Gas Appliances.	
— " —	14.7.17		— " —. V. X. Z. Batteries in action on Divisional Front.	
— " —	15.7.17		Fatigues. ——— do. ———	

2449 Wt. W14957/M90 750,000 1/16 J.B.C. & A. Forms/C.2118/12.

Army Form C. 2118.

Instructions regarding War Diaries and Intelligence Summaries are contained in F. S. Regs., Part II. and the Staff Manual respectively. Title Pages will be prepared in manuscript.

WAR DIARY
or
INTELLIGENCE SUMMARY
(Erase heading not required.)

Place	Date	Hour	Summary of Events and Information	Remarks and references to Appendices
Boiry Becquerelle.	16/7/17		Fatigues. A bombardment of FONTAINE TRENCH and SAPS was carried out from 3.0pm till 3.50pm 42 rounds 2" and 39 rounds 9.45" were fired. Timber and other material was thrown up by several rounds.	
— . —	17/7/17		Fatigues. V.Y. and Z. Batteries in action on Divisional Front.	
— . —	18/7/17		do.	
— . —	19/7/17		do.	
— . —	20/7/17		do.	
— . —	21/7/17		do.	
— . —	22/7/17		Fatigues. V.Y. & Z. Batteries in action on Divisional Front. X.50 Battery commenced preparing emplacements for 2" T. M's.	
— . —	23/7/17		Fatigues. V.Y. & Z. Batteries in action on Divisional Front. X.50 Battery continuing work on emplacements.	
— . —	24/7/17		do.	
— . —	25/7/17		A bombardment was carried out on the enemy trenches, commencing at 11.30 a.m. 14 rounds 9.45" and 20 rounds 2" were fired. Many direct hits were obtained.	
— . —	26/7/17		32 rounds 2" were fired on night of 25th/26th. in minor operations.	
— . —	27/7/17		Fatigues. V.Y. & Z. Batteries in action on Divisional Front. X.50 Battery continued work on emplacements	
— . —	28/7/17		do.	
— . —	29/7/17		do.	
— . —	30/7/17		Fatigues. V.Y. & Z Batteries in action on Divisional Front. 2 rounds 9.45" & 6 rounds 2" T.S. were fired. X.50 Battery working on emplacements	
— . —	31/7/17		Fatigues. V.Y. & Z Batteries in action on Divisional Front. X.50 Battery working on emplacements.	

[signature] Capt R.F.A.
50th Div'l T. M. Officer.

2449 Wt. W14957/M90 750,000 1/16 J.B.C. & A. Forms/C.2118/12.

Army Form C. 2118.

WAR DIARY
or
~~INTELLIGENCE SUMMARY~~ of 50th Divisional Trench Mortar Batteries.

(Erase heading not required.)

Instructions regarding War Diaries and Intelligence Summaries are contained in F. S. Regs., Part II. and the Staff Manual respectively. Title Pages will be prepared in manuscript.

August 1917 — Volume No: 14

Place	Date	Hour	Summary of Events and Information	Remarks and references to Appendices
Boiry Becquerelle.	1.8.17		Fatigues. V.Y.&Z. Batteries in action on Divisional Front. X.50 Battery working on Emplacements. V.50 Battery fired 3 rounds. 9.45"	
— " —	2/8/17		Fatigues. V.Y.&Z. Batteries in action on Divisional Front. V.50 Battery fired 15 rounds. 9.45". X.50 Battery completed 2" Emplacements.	
— " —	3/8/17		Fatigues. V.X.Y.&Z. Batteries in action on Divisional Front. X.50 Battery fired 9 rounds 2". Very good effect. Y.50 Battery fired 3 rounds 2" with temple silencer.	
— " —	4/8/17		Fatigues. V.X.Y.&Z. Batteries in action on Divisional Front. V.50 Battery fired 2 rounds 9.45" in retaliation for fishtails"	
— " —	5/8/17		Fatigues. V.X.Y.&Z. Batteries in action on Divisional Front. V.50 Battery fired 3 rounds 9.45" in retaliation for "fishtails".	
— " —	6.8.17		Fatigues. V.X.Y.&Z. Batteries in action on Divisional Front. Z.50 Battery fired 9 rounds 2" Temple Silencer in retaliation for fish-tails.	
— " —	7/8/17		Fatigues. V.X.Y.&Z Batteries in action on Divisional Front. Z.50 Battery fired 6 rounds 2" ordinary for registration.	
— " —	8/8/17		Fatigues. V.X.Y.&Z. Batteries in action on Divisional Front. V.50 Battery fired 3 rounds 9.45" in retaliation for "fish tails". Y.50 Battery fired 10 rounds 2".	
— " —	9/8/17		Fatigues. V.X.Y.&Z. Batteries in action on Divisional Front.	
— " —	10/8/17		—— do ——. V.50 Battery fired. 2 rounds 9.45" in retaliation for enemy Trench Mortars.	

2449 Wt. W14957/M90 750,000 1/16 J.B.C. & A. Forms/C.2118/12.

Instructions regarding War Diaries and Intelligence Summaries are contained in F. S. Regs., Part II. and the Staff Manual respectively. Title Pages will be prepared in manuscript.

Army Form C. 2118.

WAR DIARY
or
INTELLIGENCE SUMMARY

(Erase heading not required.)

Place	Date	Hour	Summary of Events and Information	Remarks and references to Appendices
BOIRY BECQUERELLE	11/8/17		Fatigues. V.X.Y & Z. Batteries in action on Divisional Front. In conjunction with Stokes and artillery, bombarded enemy trenches. W. of CHERISY at 10.45 pm. Mediums fired 6 rounds 2" Temple Silencer and 18 rounds 2" ordinary. Heavy fired 3. rounds 9.45".	
— " —	12/8/17		Fatigues. V.X.Y. & Z. Batteries in action on Divisional Front.	
— " —	13/8/17		——— do. ———. Y.50 Battery fired 7. rounds 2" ordinary. for registration and effect. 3 direct hits. Some timber was thrown up.	
— " —	14/8/17		Fatigues. V X Y & Z Batteries in action on Divisional Front. Y.50 Battery fired 7. rounds 2" ordinary. Three direct hits. Much timber thrown about.	
— " —	15/8/17		Fatigues. V.X.Y & Z. Batteries in action on Divisional Front. Z.50 Battery fired 6 rounds 2" ordinary. V.50 fired 3. rounds 9.45".	
— " —	16/8/17		Fatigues. V X.Y. & Z. Batteries in action on Divisional Front. V.50 fired 2 rounds 9.45" Z.50 fired 20 rounds 2" ordinary. Y.50 Battery fired 30 rounds 2" ordinary. Many direct hits were observed.	
— " —	17/8/17		Fatigues. V.X.Y. & Z. Batteries in action on Divisional Front. V.50 fired 2 rounds 9.45". Z.50 fired 20 rounds. 2" ordinary. Y.50 fired 25 rounds. 2" ordinary. Many direct hits.	
— " —	18/8/17		Fatigues. V.X.Y. & Z. Batteries in action on Divisional Front. Y.50 fired 23 rounds 2" ordinary. Z.50 Battery fired 3 rounds 2" ordinary. An exceptionally quiet night.	
— " —	19/8/17		V.X.Y. & Z. Batteries in action on Divisional Front. 3 rounds 9.45" were fired in retaliation for enemy M.W. 19 rounds 2" ordinary were fired during the night in retaliation for "fish tails," etc.	

2449 Wt. W14957/M90 750,000 1/16 J.B.C. & A. Forms/C.2118/12.

Instructions regarding War Diaries and Intelligence Summaries are contained in F. S. Regs., Part II. and the Staff Manual respectively. Title Pages will be prepared in manuscript.

WAR DIARY
or
INTELLIGENCE SUMMARY
(Erase heading not required.)

Army Form C. 2118.

Place	Date	Hour	Summary of Events and Information	Remarks and references to Appendices
BOIRY BECQUERELLE	20/[illegible]		Fatigues. V.X.Y.+Z. Batteries in action on divisional front. Heavy fired 3 rounds in retaliation for enemy M.W. Mediums fired 40 rounds 2" in retaliation for enemy [illegible].	
— " —	[illegible]		Fatigues. V.X.Y.+Z. Batteries in action on divisional front. Heavy fired [illegible] rounds. [illegible] fired 41 rounds 2" [illegible] [illegible] in retaliation for [illegible] M.W.	
— " —	[illegible]		Fatigues. V.X.Y.+Z. Batteries in action on divisional front. Heavy fired 1 round. [illegible] fired 56 rounds. 2" [illegible] in retaliation for [illegible] M.W.	
— " —	[illegible]		[illegible] V.X.Y. [illegible] Heavy fired 1 round [illegible] M.W. [illegible] fired 61 rounds [illegible]	
— " —	[illegible]		Fatigues. V.X.Y.+Z. Batteries in action on divisional front. Heavy fired [illegible] fired 41 [illegible] in retaliation for enemy [illegible] M.W. [illegible]	
— " —	[illegible]		Fatigues. V.X.Y. [illegible] Heavy fired [illegible] rounds [illegible] fired 43 rounds [illegible] M.W. [illegible]	
			[illegible] FORWARD TRENCHES. [illegible] fired 5 rounds [illegible] 17 [illegible]	
— " —	[illegible]		Fatigues. V.X.Y.+Z. [illegible] fired 31 [illegible] M.W. [illegible]	
	[illegible]		Fatigues. V.X.Y.+Z. Batteries in action on divisional front. [illegible] fired 4? [illegible] M.W. [illegible]	

2449 Wt. W14957/M90 750,000 1/16 J.B.C. & A. Forms/C.2118/12.

Army Form C. 2118.

Instructions regarding War Diaries and Intelligence Summaries are contained in F. S. Regs., Part II. and the Staff Manual respectively. Title Pages will be prepared in manuscript.

WAR DIARY
or
INTELLIGENCE SUMMARY
(Erase heading not required.)

Place	Date	Hour	Summary of Events and Information	Remarks and references to Appendices
Boiry Becquerelle.	29/8/17		Fatigues. V. X. Y. & Z. Batteries in action on Divisional Front. Heavy fired 2 rounds. Mediums fired 17 rounds. in retaliation for M.W. & G.W.	
– " –	30/8/17		A pre-arranged bombardment was successfully carried out on group of trenches round junction of CABLE and FORRARD. from 4.45 am to 5.30 am. by 4.2" and one 9.45" T.M.'s. Considerable amount of timber and wire seen scattered. Enemy retaliation was brisk at first, but was silenced by 2 rounds 2" and 2 rounds 9.45". 80 rounds 2" were fired and 17 rds 9.45" (2½ rds. expended). Long range 9.45" successfully registered. Direct hits on ST ROHART and HILLSIDE WORK. 10 rounds 2" were fired during the day.	
– " –	31/8/17		Fatigues. V. X. Y. & Z. Batteries in action on Divisional Front. Mediums fired 25 rounds 2" Heavy fired 6 rounds 9.45" on 0.32.a.65.65. An exceptionally quiet night.	

[signature]
Capt R.F.A.
50th Div. T.M. Officer.

2449 Wt. W14957/M90 750,000 1/16 J.B.C. & A. Forms/C.2118/12.

Army Form C. 2118.

Instructions regarding War Diaries and Intelligence Summaries are contained in F. S. Regs., Part II. and the Staff Manual respectively. Title Pages will be prepared in manuscript.

WAR DIARY
or
INTELLIGENCE SUMMARY OF 50TH DIVISIONAL TRENCH MORTAR BATTERIES

(Erase heading not required.)

SEPTEMBER 1917 VOLUME No 15.

21

Place	Date	Hour	Summary of Events and Information	Remarks and references to Appendices
T.1.b.1.1. BOIRY BECQUERELLE	1/9/17		V.X.Y.Z. Batteries in action on Divisional Front. Medium Batteries fired 14 rounds 2" on enemy wire and trenches in O.32.a.20.65. Heavy Battery fired 8 rounds 9.45" on O.32.a.8.4. and St ROHART in retaliation for M.W and Pistols. Observation very bad on account of slight drizzle.	
—	2/9/17		V.X.Y.Z. Batteries in action on Divisional Front. Medium Batteries fired 26 rounds 2" on enemy wire and trenches in O.32a. Many direct hits were obtained. Heavy Battery fired 13 rounds 9.45" in retaliation for enemy M.W.	
T.1.a.6.4.	3/9/17		Headquarters vacated billets at T.7.b.1.1. at 12 noon. In conjunction with 250 Brigade R.F.A. bombardment, 8 rounds 2" were fired during registration 3.–4 p.m. 20 rounds were fired from 4 pm till 5 pm. observed fire. 8 direct hits were obtained on wire, 10 direct hits on trench, 1 between trench and wire, 1 short of wire. 28 rounds also were fired on wire in front of BROWN MOUND. O.26c 4.7 to 5.4. Good results were observed.	
—	4/9/17		V.X.Y.Z. Batteries in action on Divisional Front. Medium Batteries fired 22 rounds 2" on enemy wire, in retaliation for M.W and Gas M.W. 2 rounds 9.45" were fired in retaliation for enemy M.W. and light T.M.	
—	5/9/17		26 rounds 2" were fired by the Medium Batteries. 5 rounds 9.45" were fired by the Heavy Battery on enemy wire and in retaliation for M.W. Many direct hits being obtained. Enemy also retaliated with 4.2" obtaining 3 direct hits, damaging one 2" mortar and wrecking the position.	
—	6/9/17		A pre-arranged bombardment was carried out from 5.0 – 5.45 a.m. on targets O.26.d.85.90 – O.26.d.95.00, O.32.a.[illegible], O.32.c.25.25 – O.32.c.4.2. by 2" T.M.s. 95 rounds were fired. Four rounds were duds and one round was a premature. Two casualties. Very good results and good bursts. 15 or 20 rounds must have been direct hits judging by the material thrown up. During the day 56 rounds 2" were fired by the medium batteries & 10 rds 9.45" were fired by the Heavy Battery. Good results. Several direct hits on wire were observed. Enemy retaliated with M.W. but was soon silenced.	

Army Form C. 2118.

Instructions regarding War Diaries and Intelligence Summaries are contained in F. S. Regs., Part II. and the Staff Manual respectively. Title Pages will be prepared in manuscript.

WAR DIARY
or
INTELLIGENCE SUMMARY

(Erase heading not required.)

15

Place	Date	Hour	Summary of Events and Information	Remarks and references to Appendices
T.7.a.6.4. BOIRY BECQUERELLE.	7/9/17		Medium Batteries fired 25 rds 2" & Heavy Battery fired 12 rounds 9.45" on enemy wire and in retaliation for M.W. Many direct hits were obtained on wire, and Enemy M.W. silenced.	
— " —	8/9/17		Medium Batteries fired 35 rounds 2" and Heavy Battery fired 3 rounds on enemy wire, and in retaliation for M.W. Direct hits were obtained on wire, and M.W. silenced.	
— " —	9/9/17		Medium Batteries fired 20 rounds 2". Heavy Battery fired 4 rounds 9.45" on enemy wire and in retaliation for M.W. Direct hits on wire were obtained. & M.W. silenced. An explosion was observed in enemy lines, apparently a premature from M.W.	
— " —	10/9/17		Medium Batteries fired 15 rounds 2" in retaliation for M.W. A very quiet day.	
— " —	11/9/17		Medium Batteries fired 5 rounds on O.32.a.3.4. for registration. Enemy replied with a few whizz bangs and Medium M.W. Heavy fired 3 rds 9.45" on O.32.b.1.7. in retaliation for Medium M.W.	
— " —	13/9/17		Batteries did not fire. A quiet day. Concentrated on battle positions.	
— " —	13/9/17		Heavy Battery fired 8 rounds 9.45" in retaliation. Day quiet.	
— " —	14/9/17		A pre-arranged bombardment on enemy wire was successfully carried out. 302 rounds 2" and 10 rounds 9.45" were fired, including 56 rounds 2" fired last evening to check registration. Two Very light stores were blown up. Enemy M.W and A.W reply was irregular and weak.	

2449 Wt. W14957/M90 750,000 1/16 J.B.C. & A. Forms/C.2118/12.

Army Form C. 2118.

WAR DIARY
or
INTELLIGENCE SUMMARY
(Erase heading not required.)

Instructions regarding War Diaries and Intelligence Summaries are contained in F. S. Regs., Part II. and the Staff Manual respectively. Title Pages will be prepared in manuscript.

Place	Date	Hour	Summary of Events and Information	Remarks and references to Appendices
BOIRY BECQUERELLE	15/9/17	4 pm. to 7.40 pm	A minor operation was successfully carried out on the enemy's trenches West of CHERISY. in three phases. Medium and Heavy TM's fired. Mediums fired 520 rounds in the first phase, and 280 rds in the second phase. Heavies fired 89 rds in the first phase, and 54 rds in the second phase. During the earlier part of the day. 9 rds 9.45" were fired and 66 rds 2" in retaliation for M.W's etc. Enemy silenced.	
— " —	16/9/17		Batteries did not fire. Fatigues. Cleaning pits, & mortars.	
— " —	17/9/17		— " — continued cleaning pits and mortars.	
— " —	18/9/17		Three rounds 9.45" were fired by the Heavies. 4 rounds 2" were fired by the Mediums at 4.45 pm in retaliation for M.W. Day quiet; continued work on cleaning pits etc.	
— " —	19/9/17		Two rounds 9.45" were fired at 7.30 am. in retaliation for enemy M.W. Fatigues.	
— " —	20/9/17		Three rounds 9.45" were fired in retaliation for M.W. during the day. 5 rds 9.45" and 20 rounds 2" were fired in retaliation for M.W. during the night.	
— " —	21/9/17		Six rounds 9.45" and 30 rds 2" were fired in retaliation for M.W.	
— " —	22/9/17		9 rounds 9.45" and 30 rounds 2" were fired in retaliation for M.W. A pre-arranged bombardment was carried out on Enemy Support line [illegible] to [illegible] and on M.W. Emplacement [illegible] from 6.0 – 6.45 am. 60 rounds were fired by 2" 15 rounds were fired by 9.45"; 3 rounds 2" were "duds". Considerable damage was observed in the Support line.	

2449 Wt. W14957/M90 750,000 1/16 J.B.C. & A. Forms/C.2118/12.

Army Form C. 2118.

WAR DIARY
or
INTELLIGENCE SUMMARY
(Erase heading not required.)

Instructions regarding War Diaries and Intelligence Summaries are contained in F. S. Regs., Part II. and the Staff Manual respectively. Title Pages will be prepared in manuscript.

Place	Date	Hour	Summary of Events and Information	Remarks and references to Appendices
BOIRY BECQUERELLE	23/9/17		9 rounds 9.45" and 31 rounds 2" were fired during the day. in retaliation for M.W.	
"	24/9/17		35 rounds 2" were fired during the day on enemy trenches in retaliation for M.W.	
"	25/9/17		5 rounds 9.45" were fired during the day. 49 rounds 2" were fired in retaliation for M.W.	
"	26/9/17		35 rounds 2" were fired during the day in retaliation for "Fishtails".	
"	27/9/17		54 rounds 2" were fired during the day in retaliation for M.W 11 rounds 9.45" were fired during the day on 0.32.c.5.5. and 0.26.d.9.8. in retaliation for Medium M.W. M.W. silenced.	
"	28/9/17		A pre arranged bombardment on enemy wire 0.26c.30.15 to 0.26.c.50.75. was carried out from 6.0 – 7.0 am. 152 rounds were fired by the 2" T.M.'s. A position in 0.25.b.9.0.35. was twice hit by a 4.2". The position was slightly damaged but there were no casualties. Enemy wire was badly damaged. The enemy barrage, which was put down at 6.10 am. was heavy. 40 rounds 9.45" were fired during the day. on enemy M.W's. in 0.21.b., HILLSIDE WORK and. on 0.26.d.	
"	29/9/17		26 rounds 2" were fired during the day in retaliation for Medium M.W. 11 rounds 9.45" were fired between 9.30 – 11.0 am. on SUNKEN ROADS and trenches in 0.26c and 0.32.a. in retaliation for M.W.	
"	30/9/17		61 rounds 2" were fired during the day in retaliation for Fishtails and as harassing fire on Enemy Support line. At 11.0 am 6 rounds 9.45" were fired on 0.32.b.2.8. in retaliation for M.W. Between 4.0 – 5.30pm. 9 rounds 9.45" were fired in retaliation for M.W. One of these bombs caused a fire in the enemy's lines, which burnt for a short time.	

R. Rowland[?] Capt.
a/ 50th D.T.M.O.

2449 Wt. W14957/M90 750,000 1/16 J.B.C. & A. Forms/C.2118/12.

Army Form C. 2118.

WAR DIARY
or
INTELLIGENCE SUMMARY of 50th DIVISIONAL TRENCH MORTAR BATTERIES

(Erase heading not required.)

Instructions regarding War Diaries and Intelligence Summaries are contained in F. S. Regs., Part II. and the Staff Manual respectively. Title Pages will be prepared in manuscript.

October 1917 — VOLUME No 16.

Place	Date	Hour	Summary of Events and Information	Remarks and references to Appendices
BOIRY BECQUERELLE.	1/10/17		14 rounds 9.45" and 21 rounds 2" were fired during the day in retaliation for M.W.	
T.7.a.v.4. 5.10.	2/10/17.		14 rounds 9.45" were fired on CHERRY WOOD and O.32.a.5.7. and 10 rounds were fired on HILLSIDE WORK and ST ROHARTS in retaliation for M.W. 42 rounds 2" were fired on enemy's support line. A quiet night.	
" "	3/10/17		18 rounds 9.45" were fired on HILLSIDE WORK, ST ROHARTS, and O.26.c.. 37 rounds 2" were fired during the day on enemy support line in retaliation for M.W. A pre-arranged bombardment on enemy front line U.1.b.7.8 to O.32.c.H. was carried out from 5.0 – 5.15 pm, and 6.3" 158 rounds were fired. Considerable damage was done. [illegible] [illegible] for effect bombardment was [illegible] [illegible] [illegible] [illegible] into that [illegible] behind the [illegible], but no damage was done to either mortar or personnel.	
" "	4/10/17		11 rounds 9.45" were fired during the day on O.26.b.2.0, HILLSIDE WORK, and ST ROHARTS. in retaliation for M.W. 15 rounds 2" were fired on enemy support line.	
" "	5/10/17		10 rounds 9.45" were fired on O.26 d.1.0 and HILLSIDE WORK and 40 rounds 2" were fired on O.32 a 25.15 and enemy support line in retaliation for M.W.	
" "	6/10/17		18 rounds 9.45" were fired on HILLSIDE WORK, ST ROHARTS, and M.G. emplacements in back O.26 b.8.1. 20 rounds 2" were fired on NARROW TRENCH for effect, and [illegible] rounds were fired in retaliation.	
" "	7/10/17		5 rounds 9.45" were fired on HILLSIDE WORK for effect and 4 rounds in retaliation for M.W. 25 rounds 2" were fired on NIGHT and NARROW, and FONTAINE TRENCH for effect. 27 rounds were fired on NARROW SUPPORT and SUNKEN ROAD in O.26.c. for retaliation.	
" "	8/10/17		1 rounds 9.45" were fired on H.Qrs. in CHERISY for effect and 7 rounds were fired in retaliation for M.W. Owing to high wind, it was impossible to make more use of the 9.45" this. 22 rounds 2" were fired on NARROW TRENCH and C.T's to Supports. 20 rounds 2" were fired in retaliation for M.W. during the evening.	

Instructions regarding War Diaries and Intelligence Summaries are contained in F. S. Regs., Part II. and the Staff Manual respectively. Title Pages will be prepared in manuscript.

WAR DIARY
or
INTELLIGENCE SUMMARY

(Erase heading not required.)

Army Form C. 2118.

Place	Date	Hour	Summary of Events and Information	Remarks and references to Appendices
BOIRY BECQUERELLE. T. 7.a.6.4.	9/10/17		5 rounds 9.45" were fired on HILLSIDE WORK for effect. 3 rounds were fired on H. Qrs in CHERRY WOOD for effect. 20 rounds. 2" were fired on junction of NIGHT & NARROW TRENCHES for effect. Enemy reply more brisk than usual. 4.2" being employed. 14 rounds 2" were fired on S.O.S. lines in reply to hostile M.W. Wind was too tricky to admit of more 9.45" activity.	
— " —	10/10/17		10 rounds 9.45" were fired on HILLSIDE WORK for effect. 8 rounds 9.45" were fired in reply to hostile M.W. 20 rounds 2" were fired in retaliation for M.W. Necessary repairs to pits interfering with further firing.	
— " —	11/10/17		10 rounds 9.45" were fired on H.Qrs in CHERRY WOOD for effect. 9. rounds were fired on Company H. Qrs 0.36.d. for effect. 20 rounds 2" were fired on U.1.b. 8.9. for effect. 20 rounds 2" were fired on junction of NIGHT & NARROW TRENCHES & NEVA LANE. for effect. 11 rounds 2" were fired on NARROW SUPPORT from 0.26.c. 55.10 to 0.26.c. 5.4. in retaliation for M.W.	
— " —	12/10/17		6 rounds 9.45" were fired on 0.26.d. 6.0. and 6 rounds were fired on CHERRY WOOD for effect. 10 rounds 2" were fired for registration on wire U.1.b. 7.8., 5 rounds on 0.26.a. 8.1. to check registration on wire. 20 rounds were fired on enemy front line for effect. 5 rounds were fired on enemy front line for registration. 8 rounds were fired for registration on wire U.1.b. 23 rounds were fired on trenches in U.1.b for effect. A prearranged bombardment was carried out on enemy front line 0.26.c. 4.6. to 0.26.a. 9.2. and C.T. 0.26.c. 5.7. to 0.26.a. 8.7. at 4.0 p.m. 46 rounds were fired by 9.45" This.. 240 rounds by the 2". Considerable damage was done to the enemy's trenches and a "very light" store at 0.26.c. 50.65. was blown up. During the bombardment, 10 rounds 9.45" were fired on M.W. firing from 0.32.b. 3.6. An explosion was caused, after which it ceased fire. The night was quiet.	

2449 Wt. W14957/M90 750,000 1/16 J.B.C. & A. Forms/C.2118/12.

Army Form C. 2118.

Instructions regarding War Diaries and Intelligence Summaries are contained in F. S. Regs., Part II. and the Staff Manual respectively. Title Pages will be prepared in manuscript.

WAR DIARY
or
INTELLIGENCE SUMMARY

(Erase heading not required.)

Place	Date	Hour	Summary of Events and Information	Remarks and references to Appendices
BOIRY BECQUERELLE. T.7.a.6.4.	13/10/17		9.45" fired 7 rounds on CHERRY WOOD and suspected M.W emplacement O.32.b.3.6. 2" fired 6 rounds on enemy wire U.1.b.75.90. to U.1.b.85.95. 5 rounds were fired on C.T.'s between enemy wire FONTHINE & NARROW, & 4 rounds on NIGHT & NARROW, to check registration	
— " —	14/10/17		9.45" fired 6 rounds on suspected M.W. O.32.c.9.6., 2 rounds on road junction O.27.c.80.95 and 4 rounds on H.Qrs in CHERRY WOOD for effect. 2" fired 39 rounds on enemy wire and front line O.26.c.7.7, and 40 rounds on enemy wire and front line U.1.b. for effect.	
— " —	15/10/17		9.45" fired 6 rounds on CHERRY BRIDGE for effect. 2" fired 3 rounds on enemy trenches O.26.c.4.3. 46 rounds on enemy wire and front line O.26.c.7.7 to O.26.c.4.6. for effect. 50th Divisional Trench Mortar Batteries relieved by 51st Divisional Trench Mortar Batteries at noon. Mortars were handed over at positions and personnel returned to billets.	
— " —	16/10/17		Full Marching Order Parade. Inspection of Batteries by D.T.M.O. Instructional Parade in 6" T.M's.	
— " —	17/10/17		Instructional parades in 6" T.M's. Fatigues.	
— " —	18/10/17		Route March.	
— " —	19/10/17		Route March.	
— " —	20/10/17		Foot Drill under O.s C. Batteries. Inspection Full marching order. Fatigues.	
— " —	21/10/17		Route March. Fatigues.	

2449 Wt. W14957/M90 750,000 1/16 J.B.C. & A. Forms/C.2118/12.

Army Form C. 2118.

Instructions regarding War Diaries and Intelligence Summaries are contained in F. S. Regs., Part II. and the Staff Manual respectively. Title Pages will be prepared in manuscript.

WAR DIARY
or
INTELLIGENCE SUMMARY

(Erase heading not required.)

Place	Date	Hour	Summary of Events and Information	Remarks and references to Appendices
T.7a6.4.	22/10/17		50th Divisional Trench Mortar Batteries vacated billets at T.7a6.4 and entrained for new area. at 8 – 10.30 p.m.	
	23/10/17.		Batteries detrained at PROVEN and. PESELHOEK during the morning and marched to camp at WOESTON.	
Sheet 28. WOESTON	24/10/17		Fatigues.	
– " –	25/10/17		Batteries vacated camp at WOESTON and proceeded to Forward Area B.10.d.8.4. Erection of shelters etc;	
B.10.d.8.4.	26/10/17		Fatigues. D.T.M.O and Headquarters. moved to camp at. B.15.a.2.7.	
B.15.a.2.7	27/10/17		Fatigues. Erection of huts etc.	
– " –	28/10/17		— do —	
– " –	29/10/17		— do —	
– " –	30/10/17		— do —	
– " –	31/10/17		— do —	

W.P. Johnson Lt.
for Capt R.F.A.
50th D.T.M.O.

2449 Wt. W14957/M90 750,000 1/16 J.B.C. & A. Forms/C.2118/12.

Army Form C. 2118.

Instructions regarding War Diaries and Intelligence Summaries are contained in F. S. Regs., Part II. and the Staff Manual respectively. Title Pages will be prepared in manuscript.

WAR DIARY
or
INTELLIGENCE SUMMARY of 50th Divisional Trench Mortar Batteries

(Erase heading not required.)

November 1917 Volume No. 17

Place	Date	Hour	Summary of Events and Information	Remarks and references to Appendices
B.15a.2.7	1/11/17		Fatigues, erecting dugouts etc. Salving field guns & ammunition.	
	2/11/17		— do —	
	3/11/17		— do —	
	4/11/17		— do —	
	5/11/17		— do —	
	6/11/17		— do —	
	7/11/17		— do —	
	8/11/17		— do —	
	9/11/17		— do —	
	10/11/17		— do —	
	11/11/17		— do —	
	12/11/17		— do —	
	13/11/17		— do —	
	14/11/17		— do —	
	15/11/17		— do —	
	16/11/17		— do —	
	17/11/17		— do —	
	18/11/17		— do —	
	19/11/17		— do —	

Vol 22

2449 Wt. W14957/M90 750,000 1/16 J.B.C. & A. Forms/C.2118/12.

Army Form C. 2118.

WAR DIARY
or
INTELLIGENCE SUMMARY
(Erase heading not required.)

Instructions regarding War Diaries and Intelligence Summaries are contained in F. S. Regs., Part II. and the Staff Manual respectively. Title Pages will be prepared in manuscript.

Place	Date	Hour	Summary of Events and Information	Remarks and references to Appendices
B.15.a.2.7	20/11/17		Fatigues. Y.50 Battery proceeded to Fifth Army T.M. School VALHEUREUX for course of instruction in 6" French Mortars.	
"	21/11/17		Fatigues.	
"	22/11/17		– do –	
"	23/11/17		– do –	
"	24/11/17		– do –	
"	25/11/17		– do –	
"	26/11/17		– do –	
"	27/11/17		– do –	
"	28/11/17		– do –	
"	29/11/17		– do –	
"	30/11/17		– do –	

M. McAnish [signature]
Capt R.F.A.
50th D.T.M.O.

2449 Wt. W14957/M90 750,000 1/16 J.B.C. & A. Forms/C.2118/12.

Y 50 T M Blg

Vol 4

Instructions regarding War Diaries and Intelligence Summaries are contained in F. S. Regs., Part II. and the Staff Manual respectively. Title Pages will be prepared in manuscript.

WAR DIARY
or
INTELLIGENCE SUMMARY

(Erase heading not required.)

Army Form C. 2118

Y.50 (late 29th) Trench Mortar Battery

Place	Date	Hour	Summary of Events and Information	Remarks and references to Appendices
I.24.B.5.5	31.1.16		Relieved Lt Hutchison at noon. Fired 8 rounds from B.2 from 3.7 gun at enemys front line trench during the afternoon, and 4 rounds at a Working party behind Birdcage at night.	
	1.2.16		Fired 8 rounds from 1½" gun in B.2. at enemys line from Birdcage to strong point 200 yds to right of same.	
	2.2.16		Fired 6 rounds from 3.7 at Sap on right of Birdcage. Improved 1½" position in B4 by building more cover.	
	3.2.16		Fired 12 rounds from 1½" in B4 at enemys front line opposite B.4.	
	4.2.16		Fired 9 rounds from 1½" in B2 & 8 rounds from 1½" in B4 at the same time. The gun in B2 blew up a Very light store & set off several lights	
	5.2.16		Did not fire	
	6.2.16		Was relieved by Lt Hutchison at 5 pm	

1875 Wt. W593/826 1,000,000 4/15 J.B.C. & A. A.D.S.S./Forms/C. 2118.

Instructions regarding War Diaries and Intelligence Summaries are contained in F. S. Regs., Part II. and the Staff Manual respectively. Title pages will be prepared in manuscript.

WAR DIARY
or
INTELLIGENCE SUMMARY.
(Erase heading not required.)

Army Form C. 2118.

Place	Date	Hour	Summary of Events and Information	Remarks and references to Appendices

T2134. Wt. W708—776. 500000. 4/15. Sir J. C. & S.

Army Form C. 2118

Instructions regarding War Diaries and Intelligence Summaries are contained in F. S. Regs., Part II. and the Staff Manual respectively. Title Pages will be prepared in manuscript.

WAR DIARY
or
INTELLIGENCE SUMMARY (Y 50 (Late 24th) Trench Mortar Battery.)
(Erase heading not required.)

Place	Date	Hour	Summary of Events and Information	Remarks and references to Appendices
	12.2.16		Fired 3 rounds from 2" gun in CRAB CRAWL, target being enemy's mine sap at Point J.19.c.6½.3. Registration good, receiving 2 direct hits.	
	13.2.16		All guns cleaned and ammunition brought forward to bomb stores from store in MAPLE COPSE.	
	14.2.16		At 1 am, we opened fire on point J.19.c.6½.3. firing 12 rounds 2 inch, which did considerable damage to enemy's mine sap, fire was returned at 11.30 am. by the Mae Namara.	

Instructions regarding War Diaries and Intelligence Summaries are contained in F. S. Regs., Part II. and the Staff Manual respectively. Title pages will be prepared in manuscript.

WAR DIARY

or

INTELLIGENCE SUMMARY.

(Erase heading not required.)

Army Form C. 2118.

Place	Date	Hour	Summary of Events and Information	Remarks and references to Appendices

T2134. Wt. W708–776. 500000. 4/15. Sir J. C. & S.

Army Form C. 2118.

Instructions regarding War Diaries and Intelligence Summaries are contained in F. S. Regs., Part II. and the Staff Manual respectively. Title pages will be prepared in manuscript.

WAR DIARY
or
INTELLIGENCE SUMMARY. (late 29th) Trench Mortar Batty.

(*Erase heading not required.*)

Y50

Place	Date	Hour	Summary of Events and Information	Remarks and references to Appendices
	17.2.16		In morning brought up Ammunition to B2. Went round trenches with General & Capt Hand, & decided to attack Birdcage on Saturday at 3.30 pm. In afternoon began on new sap at 3 pm. Supported by Artillery fire. Fired 23 rounds, two burst in air, nearly all the rest in the work attacked. At same time Gunner Wright in charge of mortar in B.4. fired 11 heavy & 3 light bombs. No retaliation was forthcoming in either case. There was a good deal of wind but this did not greatly effect the shooting. In the evening about 9 pm. fired 1.33lb & 2.18lb bombs from B4 in retaliation. Artillery also fired.	
	18.2.16		Prepared 2" gun emplacement all day for attack on Birdcage. Wooden bed put in. Iron girders behind with 3 2"x9" pieces under bed 1 2"x9" & 4 Concrete blocks under that. Level laterally with a slight slope forward. Arranged matters with Colonel Spain. In evening 20 more 2" bombs arrived and were stored in MAPLE COPSE. At about 11 pm being asked to retaliate took 3.7 gun up to top of GOUROCK RD, and put over 20 bombs. Various delays owing to rifle mechanism occurred till 2.15 am. Gave one rifle mechanism to Bombing Officer of 6th N.F. to give to Armourer Sergt.	

T2134. Wt. W708—776. 500000. 4/15. Sir J. C. & S.

Instructions regarding War Diaries and Intelligence Summaries are contained in F. S. Regs., Part II. and the Staff Manual respectively. Title pages will be prepared in manuscript.

WAR DIARY
or
INTELLIGENCE SUMMARY.
(Erase heading not required.)

V50 (No 29th) Trench Mortar Batty

Army Form C. 2118.

Place	Date	Hour	Summary of Events and Information	Remarks and references to Appendices
	19.2.16		Morning, Carried up ammunition for 2", Started at 3.30 pm. 12 fired, 2 duds (2"-3 1/2"). Most of work on Birdcage destroyed, Enemy wants 10 mins. to recover. In evening put 2 gunners up to work 3.7 howitz, [illegible] and myself there till 10 pm, Altogether pretty successful day.	
	20.2.16		Morning early (5 am) Visited trenches, later chose spot close to Birdcage to observe. Spent morning carrying up 2" Amm. At 2 pm. fired and considerably knocked rest of Birdcage about, of 15 fired 3 were duds. Telephone worked well, No retaliation. Also fired 6 3.7 bombs at trench opposite, many men seen to rush down trench from O.P. at in B.4. In the afternoon fired on Birdcage with 3.7 from B.4. In night 11-1 am put on range to 150 yds and got close to sap opposite end of [illegible]. Very good result as it enabled one to stop working there without shifting the gun.	
	21.2.16		Cleared up bomb stores etc in morning also fired 2 rounds with 1 1/2" from B.3 at mine enemy's trench in front. Relieved by Lt Hutchison at 11.30 am.	

Instructions regarding War Diaries and Intelligence Summaries are contained in F. S. Regs., Part II. and the Staff Manual respectively. Title Pages will be prepared in manuscript.

WAR DIARY
or
INTELLIGENCE SUMMARY (Y50 (late 29th) Trench Mortar Batty)
(Erase heading not required.)

Army Form C. 2118

Place	Date	Hour	Summary of Events and Information	Remarks and references to Appendices
	21.2.16		Relieved by Lt MacNamara at 11.30 am.	
			Fired 6 rounds 3.7 at Birdcage and new Sap in front of B.2.	
			Selected new 2" emplacement after a careful survey of all ground.	
			Commenced building new position in support line, between CRAB CRAWL and ST. PETERS ST. (I.24.D.6.3).	
			During the night 6 rounds 3.7 fired on Birdcage, and new sap in front of B.2.	
	22.2.16		Continued work all day until midnight on new 2" position.	
			Fired 5 rounds 3.7 in retaliation to rifle Grenades which fell behind B4. the shoot being effective as no more rifle Grenades were sent over.	
			6 Rounds 3.7 fired into enemy's new sap from trench A.10 during the night.	

Instructions regarding War Diaries and Intelligence Summaries are contained in F. S. Regs., Part II. and the Staff Manual respectively. Title pages will be prepared in manuscript.

WAR DIARY

or

INTELLIGENCE SUMMARY.

(Erase heading not required.)

Army Form C. 2118.

Place	Date	Hour	Summary of Events and Information	Remarks and references to Appendices

T2134. Wt. W708—776. 500000. 4/15. Sir J. C. & S.

Instructions regarding War Diaries and Intelligence Summaries are contained in F. S. Regs., Part II. and the Staff Manual respectively. Title Pages will be prepared in manuscript.

WAR DIARY
or
INTELLIGENCE SUMMARY Y50 (late 29) Trench Mortar Bty

(*Erase heading not required.*)

Army Form C. 2118

Place	Date	Hour	Summary of Events and Information	Remarks and references to Appendices
	28/2/16		Took over from Lt Hutchison at 11-0 am. Fired on trenches opposite A.9 and B.3 with 3.7 gun.	
	29/2/16		Fired at Snipers post near Birdcage from Mortar in B.4 (6 rounds) 33 pdr. Afternoon fired on trenches opposite B.4 with 3.7 gun (6 rounds.	
			Alexander Hutchison Lieut Y.50 (late 29) Trench Mortar Battery 50th Division	

1875 Wt. W593/826 1,000,000 4/15 J.B.C. & A. A.D.S.S./Forms/C. 2118.

Army Form C. 2118.

Instructions regarding War Diaries and Intelligence Summaries are contained in F. S. Regs., Part II. and the Staff Manual respectively. Title Pages will be prepared in manuscript.

WAR DIARY
or
INTELLIGENCE SUMMARY

(Erase heading not required.)

Place	Date	Hour	Summary of Events and Information	Remarks and references to Appendices

2449 Wt. W14957/M00 750,000 1/16 J.B.C. & A. Forms/C.2118/12.

Instructions regarding War Diaries and Intelligence Summaries are contained in F. S. Regs., Part II. and the Staff Manual respectively. Title Pages will be prepared in manuscript.

WAR DIARY
or
INTELLIGENCE SUMMARY of Y.50 Trench Mortar Battery

(Erase heading not required.)

Army Form C. 2118.

Place	Date	Hour	Summary of Events and Information	Remarks and references to Appendices
	9/4/16	5	Work continued on all emplacements. Fired 9 rounds of 2" on Front line of Bois Quarante at 5 pm + later fired 3 rounds of 18 Pdr in retaliation for Fish Tail.	
	10/4/16		Work commenced on 2" emplacement in M1 Bay 18 Detachment relieved, all guns cleaned Gunner Pearce wounded in fingers	
	11/4/16		Work continued on M1 2" 1½ bomb store in Jarvis St. cleaned out + arranged for instant action	
	12/4/16		Fetched Ammunition from P2. Fused Ammunition for 1½" & 2" + fetched O3 gun to Concrete Bed Bombstore. Cleaned out Concrete Bed where it was hit by 5.9" H E shell.	
	13/4/16		Carried material to O1 position fired 3 rounds 2" at sap O7 b 35 from O3 2" gun at 6.30 Pm	

2449 Wt. W14957/M90 750,000 1/16 J.B.C. & A. Forms/C.2118/12.

Army Form C. 2118.

Instructions regarding War Diaries and Intelligence Summaries are contained in F. S. Regs., Part II. and the Staff Manual respectively. Title Pages will be prepared in manuscript.

WAR DIARY
or
INTELLIGENCE SUMMARY

(Erase heading not required.)

Place	Date	Hour	Summary of Events and Information	Remarks and references to Appendices

2449 Wt. W14957/M90 750,000 1/16 J.B.C. & A. Forms/C.2118/12.

Instructions regarding War Diaries and Intelligence Summaries are contained in F. S. Regs., Part II. and the Staff Manual respectively. Title Pages will be prepared in manuscript.

WAR DIARY
or
INTELLIGENCE SUMMARY of Y.50 Trench Mortar Battery

(Erase heading not required.)

Army Form C. 2118.

Place	Date	Hour	Summary of Events and Information	Remarks and references to Appendices
	April 17		Relieved 2/Lt Godley	
	18 19 20 21		Fired daily in retaliation to enemy mortars silencing the enemy on every occasion – Fire was concentrated on enemy front line opposite 81 A – his parapet was practically wiped out for 30 yards or more – some shots fell in his wire & some in rear of his front trench – I fired from 2 inch & 1½ inch – On one occasion I also fired in retaliation for his shelling of M & N Trenches. On 20th the Bosche tried to wipe out 2 inch gun here situated in rear of 81A firing about 270 5.9 shells into a space about 60 x 80 yds – he did not hit the gun or bomb stores but destroyed my dugout & with it my War Diary which I had kept daily	
	21		I was wounded.	

W Bennett Lieut.
T.M. Bde 56th Division

2449 Wt. W14957/M90 750,000 1/16 J.B.C. & A. Forms/C.2118/12.

Instructions regarding War Diaries and Intelligence Summaries are contained in F. S. Regs., Part II. and the Staff Manual respectively. Title pages will be prepared in manuscript.

Army Form C. 2118.

WAR DIARY

or

INTELLIGENCE SUMMARY. of Y50 Trench Mortar Battery

(Erase heading not required.)

Place	Date	Hour	Summary of Events and Information	Remarks and references to Appendices
	22/7/16		Fired 6 rounds from 2" gun in O.2 at 2 am in retaliation to enemy Mortars considerable damage done to enemys Parapet. Remainder of day quiet.	
	23/7/16		Fired 12 rounds from 1½" gun in O.1.A at 7 am in retaliation to enemy Mortars. During the day position were improved. Registered 1½" gun in O.1.A on several points of enemys line. Remainder of day very quiet. Relieved by [illegible] Battery at 5 pm	

T2134. Wt. W708–776. 500000. 4/15. Sir J. C. & S.

Instructions regarding War Diaries and Intelligence Summaries are contained in F. S. Regs., Part II. and the Staff Manual respectively. Title Pages will be prepared in manuscript.

WAR DIARY
or
INTELLIGENCE SUMMARY of Y.50 Trench Mortar Battery

(Erase heading not required.)

Army Form C. 2118.

Place	Date	Hour	Summary of Events and Information	Remarks and references to Appendices
	24/4/16		Commenced to take 1½" guns out of action. About 12.15 p.m Enemy opened fire with shells (probably 5.9") on support trenches followed by Trench Mortars one of which was a large Minenwerfer on our front trench. Retaliated with 1½" on Enemy's front line some of which smashed in enemy's parapet. Ceased firing about 1.30. p.m remainder of day quiet	
	25/4/16		Completed taking 1½ guns out of action. Two 2" guns brought in. Enemy again active with shells & Trench Mortars. Large Minenwerfer was again in action. Commenced to put 2" gun in Jarvis St.	
	26/4/16		Continued on 2" emplacements. About 1 p.m Enemy again used his Trench Mortars. Retaliated with 2". Fired seven rounds on to Enemy's Support Trenches which must have caused some damage to his Trenches as he ceased to fire his Mortars. About 10 p.m a bombing attack commenced just on our left. Fired one 2" bomb but as attack was not directed against us we ceased firing	

2449 Wt. W14957/M90 750,000 1/16 J.B.C. & A. Forms/C.2118/12.

Army Form C. 2118.

Instructions regarding War Diaries and Intelligence Summaries are contained in F. S. Regs., Part II. and the Staff Manual respectively. Title pages will be prepared in manuscript.

WAR DIARY
or
INTELLIGENCE SUMMARY.

(Erase heading not required.)

Place	Date	Hour	Summary of Events and Information	Remarks and references to Appendices

T2131. Wt. W708–776. 500000. 4/15. Sir J. C. & S.

Instructions regarding War Diaries and Intelligence Summaries are contained in F. S. Regs., Part II. and the Staff Manual respectively. Title pages will be prepared in manuscript.

WAR DIARY
or
INTELLIGENCE SUMMARY. of Y.50 Trench Mortar Battery
(Erase heading not required.)

Army Form C. 2118.

Place	Date	Hour	Summary of Events and Information	Remarks and references to Appendices
	29/4/16		Morning fairly quiet. All gun emplacements improved. Fired three rounds 2" from Jarvis Street C.T. at 9 am. & one from position N.2.R. & N.3. About 11-45 enemy started with trench mortars, again using his large minenwerfer, but in a different direction, only two rounds were fired. Retaliated with 2" from Jarvis Street C.T. fired eight rounds on to enemy support. About 4 pm. enemy shelled BOIS CARRE C.T. with a small field gun. At 6.45 enemy sent over several rounds of shrapnel in rear of N.4 & 5. Our Artillery replied effectively.	
	30/4/16		About 2 am. enemy opened fire with trench mortars & shells. Retaliated with 2", fired eight rounds. At 9.30 am enemy again fired several rounds. We then fired four rounds from gun in Jarvis Street C.T. which landed in enemy's support trenches, much damage being done, and enemy ceased fire. Retaliated at 4.30 pm to enemy trench mortars. During the afternoon enemy shelled O2. & O3 supports with 5.9 howitz. Relieved by 3rd Div. Trench Mortar Bde at 8 pm, Relief completed by 8.45 pm.	

T.S. Corder 2nd Lt R.F.A
for Cmdg Y.50 Trench Mortar Bty

T2134. Wt. W708—776. 500000. 4/15. Sir J. C. & S.

Instructions regarding War Diaries and Intelligence Summaries are contained in F. S. Regs., Part II. and the Staff Manual respectively. Title pages will be prepared in manuscript.

WAR DIARY
or
INTELLIGENCE SUMMARY. of Y.50 Trench Mortar Battery

(Erase heading not required.)

Army Form C. 2118.

Vol 3

Place	Date	Hour	Summary of Events and Information	Remarks and references to Appendices
Q 28 d 1.7	1/5/16	9am	Proceeded with party of men to [illegible].	
"	2/5/16	6.30–12.30	Training. Route March, Gun drill, Semaphore.	
"	3/5/16	9am–12.30	Training. Gun drill, Telephony, preparing 2" gun positions.	
"	4/5/16	" "	Training Preparing 2" gun position, Semaphore, 2" Gun drill	
"	5/5/16	"	Fatigues.	
"	7/5/16	"	Church Parade, Rifle inspection.	
"	8/5/16	9am–6pm	Training. 2" gun drill, Semaphore, preparing 2" gun position, Baths.	
"	9/5/16	12.30pm	Training. Telephony.	
"	10/5/16	"	Training. 2" Gun drill, Semaphore, Squad drill with rifles	
"	11/5/16	"	Training. 2" Gun drill, Telephony, Rifle drill	
"	12/5/16	"	Training. Preparing 2" gun position, Semaphore.	
"	13/5/16	"	Training. Gun drill, Telephony, Musketry.	
"	14/5/16		Rifle inspection, Church Parade.	
"	15/5/16	"	Training, Gun drill with tube helmets, Semaphore, Musketry.	
"	16/5/16	"	Training Telephony. Tube helmet drill, Gun drill.	
"	17/5/16	"	Training Semaphore. Gun drill. Musketry.	

T/131. Wt. W708–776. 500,000. 4/15. Sir J. C. & S.

Army Form C. 2118.

Instructions regarding War Diaries and Intelligence Summaries are contained in F. S. Regs., Part II. and the Staff Manual respectively. Title pages will be prepared in manuscript.

WAR DIARY
or
INTELLIGENCE SUMMARY. of Y.50 Trench Mortar Bty

(Erase heading not required.)

Place	Date	Hour	Summary of Events and Information	Remarks and references to Appendices
Q.28 d 1.7.	18/5/16	9am–12.30pm	Fatigues.	
	19/5/16	" "	Training. Gun drill. Semaphore. Musketry	
	20/5/16	"	Training Gun drill. Telephony. preparing 2" gun position	
	21/5/16	9.30am	Church Parade	
	22/5/16	9–12.30pm	Fatigues,	
	23/5/16		Sports.	
	24/5/16	9am–12.30pm	Fatigues.	
	25/5/16		Proceeded to LOCRE, then to the trenches, where I was shown gun positions and targets, returned to billet at 7 pm.	
	26/5/16		Relieved Lt Snape of X3 T.M.B. about 11 pm, situation quiet during night.	
	27/5/16	9am	At 9am work started on 2" Emplacement in trench N3, where a sand bag wall was built round the gun.	
		2pm	2 Rounds 2" fired on point N.12.d.9.7 in retaliation for Sausages. Enemy effectively silenced	
		9pm	Received Ammunition, and conveyed same to bomb stores in front line trench.	

T2134. Wt. W708–776. 500000. 4/15. Sir J. C. & S.

Instructions regarding War Diaries and Intelligence Summaries are contained in F. S. Regs., Part II. and the Staff Manual respectively. Title pages will be prepared in manuscript.

WAR DIARY

or

INTELLIGENCE SUMMARY.

(Erase heading not required.)

Army Form C. 2118.

Place	Date	Hour	Summary of Events and Information	Remarks and references to Appendices

Instructions regarding War Diaries and Intelligence Summaries are contained in F. S. Regs., Part II. and the Staff Manual respectively. Title pages will be prepared in manuscript.

WAR DIARY
or
INTELLIGENCE SUMMARY. of Y.50 Trench M. Bty

(Erase heading not required.)

Army Form C. 2118.

Place	Date	Hour	Summary of Events and Information	Remarks and references to Appendices
	31/5/16	3am	4 rounds fired on O.7.C.1.5 in retaliation for Rum Jars. Much damage done to enemy trenches.	
	"	3.30am	7 rounds fired on O.7.C.4.93 which caused much damage to new work in Crater.	
			Continued work on new Emplacements.	
		2pm	23 rounds fired on O.7.B.6.1 in retaliation for Rum Jars & Minnenwerfer. Enemy silenced.	

A Hutchison Lt.
O.C. Y.50 T.M. Battery

T2134. Wt. W708–776. 500000. 4/15. Sir J. C. & S.

Instructions regarding War Diaries and Intelligence Summaries are contained in F. S. Regs., Part II. and the Staff Manual respectively. Title Pages will be prepared in manuscript.

WAR DIARY
or
INTELLIGENCE SUMMARY of Y 50 Trench Mortar Bty.
(Erase heading not required.)

Army Form C. 2118.

Vol 6

Place	Date	Hour	Summary of Events and Information	Remarks and references to Appendices
N2	1/6/16	–	Continued work on N2 position.	
—	"	–	All gun pieces & [illegible] are returned to H.Q. one new gun complete received in exchange – Situation normal	
	2/6/16	–	Continued work on all positions, Ammunition carried to [illegible] in front line from [illegible] at [illegible]	
O7a 8.1 O7a 7.5	3/6/16	–	Continued work on new positions. At midday, 9TM destroyed several dugouts in N6 but were silenced after 7 rounds fired from N2. Ammunition carried by [illegible] during the night	
O1d 6.2	4/6/16	–	Continued work on new position. Situation very quiet.	
		3pm	Lt Godley relieved Lt Hutchinson	
N6c 8.1	5/6/16		Work commenced on [illegible] & Bois Carré – Ammunition carried to front line	
N6c 8.1	6/6/16		Work continued on [illegible] & Bois Carré	
O7a 7.5	7/6/16		Fired 10 rounds from O7 position on Enemy Crater at O7a 6.4 with 21 rounds from N2 gun on N12 9.0. Enemy retaliated with [illegible] & [illegible]	
O7a 6.5	8/6/16		Took gun out of [illegible] and cleaned it – defended position	
O7a 8.1	9/6/16		Fired 9 rounds in retaliation to point N12 9.0 continued work on [illegible]	
O7a 7.5	10/6/16		Fired 10 rounds in retaliation from O7 gun on O7c 1.9 and damaged the trench – Commenced work [illegible] Complement.	
N12 9.8	11/6/16		Put in gun at N2 Bay 8/10 commenced new crater at Hollandscheschuur [illegible]. Lt Hutchinson relieved Lt Godley – No firing.	
O7a 7.5	12/6/16		During [illegible] conditions at [illegible] at 1.3pm E.7.11 fired [illegible] but were silenced by 6 rounds on point O7d 2.6	

2449 Wt. W14957/M90 750,000 1/16 J.B.C. & A. Forms/C.2118/12.

Instructions regarding War Diaries and Intelligence Summaries are contained in F. S. Regs., Part II. and the Staff Manual respectively. Title Pages will be prepared in manuscript.

WAR DIARY
or
INTELLIGENCE SUMMARY of Y50 Trench Mortar Bty.

(Erase heading not required.)

Army Form C. 2118.

Place	Date	Hour	Summary of Events and Information	Remarks and references to Appendices
O1 d 42	13/6/16		Situation quiet, no firing. Fresh position started in P&O trench at point O1 D42.	
O1 d 42 / N12 d 98	14/6/16		Continued work on new position in P&O trench. At 2.00 pm E.T.M. fired on M&M trenches. We retaliated with N2 gun on Crater N12 d 29 and after firing 7 rounds the T.M. shifted on to trench fire. Opened fire with N3 gun & fired 10 rounds. E.T.M. was silenced. Bois CARRE heavily shelled from 2.30 till 4.20 pm.	
O1 d 42	15/6/16		Continued work on new position at O1 D42 in P&O Trench. At 4.20 pm fired 2 rounds from N2 gun on Crater at N12 D29, fired 4 rounds in retaliation to E.T.M. at point O7 D1 28 which was silenced. Quiet night.	
O1 d 42 / O7 a 1.1	16/6/16		Continued work on P&O. position. At 8 pm fired 9 rounds from N3 on O7 d 29 in retaliation to E.T.M. which was silenced.	
	17/6/16		Continued work on P&O Trench. Strengthened N2 position. No firing.	
N12 d 98	18/6/16		Continued work on P&O Trench and N2 position. Bombstore rebuilt. At 11 am fired 3 rounds from N2 on Crater N12 D29. 2Lt Godley relieved Lt Hutchinson at 4 pm.	
O1 d 42	19/6/16		Continued work in Bois Confluent. No firing.	
O1 d 42 / O7 c 75	20/6/16		Continued work in Bois Confluent, Continued work at Jarvis St, at 12.30 pm fired 14 rounds from O1 gun in retaliation on O7 c 69	
O1 d 42	21/6/16		Continued work in Bois Confluent, fired 13 rounds from O1 in retaliation to E.T.M. on O7 c 69	
O7 a 1.1 / O7 c 75 / O7 a 1.1	22/6/16		Gunner Parton wounded. Fired 27 rounds from N1A on O7 a 92, and 11 from O1 on to point O7 c 69, E.T.M. retaliated. Continued Bois Confluent Position. Drained N3 position.	

2449 Wt. W14957/M90 750,000 1/16 J.B.C. & A. Forms/C.2118/12.

Instructions regarding War Diaries and Intelligence Summaries are contained in F. S. Regs., Part II. and the Staff Manual respectively. Title Pages will be prepared in manuscript.

WAR DIARY
or
INTELLIGENCE SUMMARY
(Erase heading not required.)

Army Form C. 2118.

Place	Date	Hour	Summary of Events and Information	Remarks and references to Appendices

2449 Wt. W14957/M90 750,000 1/16 J.B.C. & A. Forms/C.2118/12.

Instructions regarding War Diaries and Intelligence Summaries are contained in F. S. Regs., Part. II. and the Staff Manual respectively. Title Pages will be prepared in manuscript.

WAR DIARY
or
~~INTELLIGENCE SUMMARY~~
(Erase heading not required.)

Army Form C. 2118

24th Trench Mortar Battery

Imp. Hav., 26/7 — 10.000

Place	Date	Hour	Summary of Events and Information	Remarks and references to Appendices
In the Field	30/11/15		I relieved 2/Lt. A. Hutchison at 7 P.M. & did no firing during the night	
	1/12/15		In accordance with instructions received, no firing was done	
	2/12/15		No firing was done.	
			I was relieved at 6.45 P.M. by 2/Lt. E. G. Porter	
			[signature] 2/Lt.	
			29th Battery T.M. Brigade	

Army Form C. 2118

Instructions regarding War Diaries and Intelligence Summaries are contained in F. S. Regs., Part. II. and the Staff Manual respectively. Title Pages will be prepared in manuscript.

WAR DIARY

or

~~INTELLIGENCE SUMMARY~~

(Erase heading not required.)

Imp. Hav., 26/7 — 10,000

Place	Date	Hour	Summary of Events and Information	Remarks and references to Appendices
In the Field	30/11/15		I relieved 2/Lt A. Hutchison at 7. P.M. + did not fire during the night	
	1/12/15		In accordance with instructions received, no firing was done	
	2/12/15		No firing was done	[illegible]
			I was relieved at 6.45 P.M. by 2/Lt. E. G. Porter	
			[illegible signature] 2/Lt.	
			29th Battery. T. M. Brigade	

Instructions regarding War Diaries and Intelligence Summaries are contained in F. S. Regs., Part II. and the Staff Manual respectively. Title Pages will be prepared in manuscript.

WAR DIARY
or
INTELLIGENCE SUMMARY
(Erase heading not required.)

29th Trench Mortar Battery

Army Form C. 2118

Place	Date	Hour	Summary of Events and Information	Remarks and references to Appendices
Belgium	19.12.15		29th T.M. Bty received orders to report to 50th Div. for duty.	
	20.12.15		2/Lt Hutchinson visits 9th Div area & takes over guns & ammunition belonging to this Division.	
	21.12.15		2/Lt Cameron goes into action in Sanctuary Wood with 10 N.C.O's & men. Find ammunition & stores in unsatisfactory condition & after consultation with [illegible] Infantry Brigade 151, decides to occupy time in building new emplacements & effectively dealing with guns & stores. No firing was done.	[illegible] 7/1/16
	27.12.15		No firing during the week. Time spent as above. Relieved by 3/1st Trench	

[illegible signature]

1875 Wt. W593/826 1,000,000 4/15 J.B.C. & A. A.D.S.S./Forms/C. 2118.

Instructions regarding War Diaries and Intelligence Summaries are contained in F. S. Regs., Part II. and the Staff Manual respectively. Title Pages will be prepared in manuscript.

WAR DIARY
~~or~~
~~INTELLIGENCE SUMMARY~~
(Erase heading not required.)

Army Form C. 2118

Place	Date	Hour	Summary of Events and Information	Remarks and references to Appendices
Sheet 28.			I relieved 2/Lt D. Grant at mid-day 10th January.	
I.24.D.55	10.1.16.		During the afternoon I received orders from the General to fire at snipers post in front of B.4. after firing 2 rounds it had the desired effect. the sniper being dislodged.	
	11.1.16		It was reported that sniper had returned, and was sniping from new position to the left of former. I took up new position in left of B.4. from where I fired 10 rounds 4 inch. and succeeded in a direct hit, the trench being badly damaged. During afternoon I had party of men working at new 2 inch gun position in CRAB.CRAWL trench.	
	12.1.16		It was reported that new wire had been placed round BIRDCAGE also a working party had been seen building up new sandbags. From 4 inch gun in B2. 5 rounds were fired all of which were most effective blowing up wire and sandbags. Continued work at 2 inch gun position also at MAPLE COPSE bomb store.	

1875 Wt. W593/826 1,000,000 4/15 J.B.C. & A. A.D.S.S./Forms/C. 2118.

Army Form C. 2118

Instructions regarding War Diaries and Intelligence Summaries are contained in F. S. Regs., Part II. and the Staff Manual respectively. Title Pages will be prepared in manuscript.

WAR DIARY
~~or~~
~~INTELLIGENCE SUMMARY~~

(Erase heading not required.)

Place	Date	Hour	Summary of Events and Information	Remarks and references to Appendices
	13-1-16		During the day that ammunition shifted to new bomb store in MAPLE COPSE. Also all guns cleaned and well oiled.	
	14-1-16 15-1-16		Building new dug-out for men in MAPLE COPSE.	
	16-1-16		Continued work at 2 inch gun position. I was relieved by 2/Lt Grant at 4 pm. 16-1-16.	
			Alexander Hutchison 2/Lt. 29th Trench Mortar Battery. 58th Division	

1875 Wt. W593/826 1,000,000 4/15 J.B.C. & A. A.D.S.S./Forms/C. 2118.

Instructions regarding War Diaries and Intelligence Summaries are contained in F. S. Regs., Part II. and the Staff Manual respectively. Title pages will be prepared in manuscript.

WAR DIARY

or

INTELLIGENCE SUMMARY.

(Erase heading not required.)

Army Form C. 2118.

Place	Date	Hour	Summary of Events and Information	Remarks and references to Appendices

T2134. Wt. W708—776. 500000. 4/15. Sir J. C. & S.

Instructions regarding War Diaries and Intelligence Summaries are contained in F. S. Regs., Part II. and the Staff Manual respectively. Title pages will be prepared in manuscript.

WAR DIARY

or

~~INTELLIGENCE SUMMARY.~~

(Erase heading not required.)

Army Form C. 2118.

Place	Date	Hour	Summary of Events and Information	Remarks and references to Appendices
	23/4/16		impossible to see exactly where it fell. I then switched on to J 19 c 4.7½ + got a direct hit on the enemy's parapet after two shots had gone over it.	
	24/4/16	1.pm	I was relieved by 2/Lt A. Hutchison.	
			I was prevented from firing the 1½ + 4 inch guns owing to lack of ammunition for the 4 inch + fuzes for the 1½ inch. The latter were repeatedly asked for but without success. It was particularly unfortunate not being able to fire the 1½ inch guns as there are several strong points which could easily be engaged + which are growing in number + strength. These strong points are too close to our line to be engaged by artillery + with sufficient Trench Mortar ammunition we could have prevented them being built, as they have been without any opposition.	
			[illegible] 2/Lt 29th Trench Mortar Battery	

Instructions regarding War Diaries and Intelligence Summaries are contained in F. S. Regs., Part II. and the Staff Manual respectively. Title pages will be prepared in manuscript.

WAR DIARY

~~or~~

~~INTELLIGENCE SUMMARY.~~

(Erase heading not required.)

Army Form C. 2118.

Place	Date	Hour	Summary of Events and Information	Remarks and references to Appendices
I·24·D·55 Sheet 28.	24·1·16		I relieved 2/Lt Grant at mid-day 24th January. No firing.	
	25·1·16		I had working party building sandbags round 1½ inch gun position in left of B·4. trench.	
	26·1·16		During forenoon I fired 6 rounds (registration) from 1½ inch gun in B·4, the effect being good, blowing up dug-out and part of enemy's trench.	
	27·1·16		From 1½ gun in B·2. I fired 4 rounds (registration) all rounds being effective also registration good. During afternoon I had some stores replenished from store in MAPLE COPSE.	
	28·1·16		From 1½ inch gun in B·4. 2 rounds were fired for demonstration the effect was good, blowing lots of timber in the air from roof of enemy's dug-out in front line trench.	

T2134. Wt. W708—776. 500000. 4/15. Sir J. C. & S.

Instructions regarding War Diaries and Intelligence Summaries are contained in F. S. Regs., Part II. and the Staff Manual respectively. Title pages will be prepared in manuscript.

WAR DIARY

~~or~~

~~INTELLIGENCE SUMMARY.~~

(Erase heading not required.)

Army Form C. 2118.

Place	Date	Hour	Summary of Events and Information	Remarks and references to Appendices
	29.1.16		A reserve position was made for 1½ gun in B.3.S. trench.	
	30.1.16		All guns and stores thoroughly cleaned, and oiled, also trench boards put down in trench leading to 2 inch position in CRAB CRAWL trench.	
	31.1.16.		At 9.45.am. from behind BIRDCAGE the enemy sent over 2 trench mortar shells, which landed at top of GOUROCK ROAD, one being a dud, the other doing little damage. From 1½ inch gun in B.2. I fired 8 rounds, with Artillery support; causing considerable damage to trenches.	
			I was relieved at mid-day by 2/Lt. D. Grant.	
			Alexander Hutcheson 2/Lt. 29th Trench Mortar Battery 50th Division	

T2134. Wt. W708—776. 500000. 4/15. Sir J. C. & S.

99 Trench Motor Bty
Jan
Vol I

Instructions regarding War Diaries and Intelligence Summaries are contained in F. S. Regs., Part II. and the Staff Manual respectively. Title Pages will be prepared in manuscript.

WAR DIARY
or
INTELLIGENCE SUMMARY
(Erase heading not required.)

Army Form C. 2118

_APPENDIX. 13

2G Trench Battery

Place	Date	Hour	Summary of Events and Information	Remarks and references to Appendices
In the Field	19/6/15		Proceeded to Farm H q. d. 9.2 as advised by DA 14th Division & arrived at Farm at 4 p.m. Reported DA at 5 o'clock & [illegible] Battery to D.A to-morrow so as to be in closer touch for [illegible]. Farm H q d. 9.2 being two miles from D.A.	
	20/6/15		DA arranging transport. Brought Battery to D.A at 3 P.m. Received orders at 12.15 p.m to report at H.Q 5th Oxford & Buck L.I. (42 Infantry Bde) at 4 o'clock p.m. Borrowed bicycle & reported & spent till 7.30 p.m reconnoitring the Trenches for position for Battery. Very difficult as 1st line Trenches [illegible] only 20 to 30 yds from enemy. Finally settled on position in communication Trenches for two guns. Reported to D.A at 10 p.m who agreed that we should place ½ the Battery in position to-morrow night as suggested by 42 Infantry Bde. D.A arranging [illegible] horse transport to meet fatigue of 25 men from Infantry to [illegible] [illegible] 2 guns & 1 spare bed & 52 rounds of ammunition through trenches to Battery position after dark to-morrow – the rest of the Battery to remain at D.A	
	21/6/15		arranged with S.S.O of 14th Division to send rations to D.A in future & that we should be attached to D.A for rations & to repay Infantry Bde at refilling point for rations for the 12 men in the Trenches. Reported DA the difficulty as to suitable positions in these trenches [illegible] position must be 150 yds at least behind the target & pointed out the Target on [illegible] Trench map.	
		9 P.m	Left D.A & reached [illegible] at 9-30 when we found that 30 men at least were required to carry our Bombs. We managed to procure 6 more men to help & even then we should have hardly been able to manage it had we not met with further assistance from infantry passing us in the Trenches. With 50 men we were required to carry half the Battery with 52 Bombs in addition to our own 11 men. (for distances over a mile) we reached the Trenches of the 43 Infantry Bde at 1.15 A.M. Owing to orders that I was not to place my guns within 150 yds of target (Redoubt) I made a further reconnaissance at day break [illegible] as such a position was difficult to find. Decided upon one in communication Trenches	
	22/6			

1875 Wt. W593/826 1,000,000 4/15 J.B.C. & A. A.D.S.S./Forms/C. 2118.

Army Form C. 2118

Instructions regarding War Diaries and Intelligence Summaries are contained in F. S. Regs., Part II. and the Staff Manual respectively. Title Pages will be prepared in manuscript.

WAR DIARY
or
INTELLIGENCE SUMMARY
(Erase heading not required.)

Place	Date	Hour	Summary of Events and Information	Remarks and references to Appendices
[illegible]	[illegible]		[illegible]	

1875 Wt. W503/826 1,000,000 4/15 J.B.C. & A. A.D.S.S./Forms/C. 2118.

Instructions regarding War Diaries and Intelligence Summaries are contained in F. S. Regs., Part II. and the Staff Manual respectively. Title Pages will be prepared in manuscript.

WAR DIARY
or
INTELLIGENCE SUMMARY
(Erase heading not required.)

Army Form C. 2118

Place	Date	Hour	Summary of Events and Information	Remarks and references to Appendices
In the Field	23/6		During early morning enemy continued their gun fire. At 8 AM I again reported to the O.C. 42nd Bde & asked him if he wished me to fire when he said he did not want me to fire at all to-day unless there were further developments in the situation. At 11 AM I wrote a report of what had been done to D.A. & sent S. Sr Archer with report & advised him to rest at D.A. until I ordered his return to the Trenches. I also sent a short report to the Commandant 4.30 an interview [illegible] the O.C. 43rd Bde who were relieving the 42nd Bde to-morrow & arranged with him	X that I should have a telephone to a better observing station
	24/6	10 AM	Received communication from D.A. that I was being relieved. I reported to O.C. 42 Bde for orders who said he did not want me to fire to-day as the Infantry were being relieved that night so he wished all to be quiet till this was done	
		12 midday	Capt Beerbohm arrived to relieve me. I handed over to him & took him round the Trenches & showed him the gun positions of the Redoubt. I left Trenches at 1.45 PM & reported at H.Q. 14th D.A. at 4.30 PM	

Instructions to O.C.29th.Trench Howitzer Batt.

1.In confirmation of instructions given you last night you will bomb the redoubt at the E.corner of RAILWAY WOOD during the two ten minute bombardments at 7.30-7.40pm.and at 7.50 to 8.pm.

2.When the assault takes place you will get in touch with the Officer Commanding Oxford and Bucks L.I.and co-operate with him as the situation demands.

Bde Major R.A.

14th.Div.

12 Noon.

22/6/15.

Army Form C. 2118

WAR DIARY
or
~~INTELLIGENCE SUMMARY~~
(Erase heading not required.)

Instructions regarding War Diaries and Intelligence Summaries are contained in F. S. Regs., Part II. and the Staff Manual respectively. Title Pages will be prepared in manuscript.

29th Trench. M Bty. 14th Div.

Place	Date	Hour	Summary of Events and Information	Remarks and references to Appendices
Ypres.	1.7.15		Out of action. ~~Sent~~ all heavy bombs to BERTHEN as ordered by C.R.A.	
	2.7.15	11 p.m.	Ordered into action.	
Railway Wood (Ypres-Roulers Ry)	3.7.15		Mounted gun in new position in RAILWAY WOOD. Fired two rounds at redoubt S.E. of our barrier on RAILWAY known as Y7. The range being 170 yds both were air bursts. Reported to C.R.A. that light bombs give air bursts at ranges under 200 yds & that I could not fire again at this target till heavy bombs are supplied. Fired five rounds at redoubt E. of RAILWAY WOOD, all of which took effect.	
	4.7.15		Fired 8 rounds at this redoubt 5 of which were effective. One blind, two air bursts.	
	5.7.15		At about 10.30 a.m. enemy occupied our barrier on the Railway after bombarding it for about ½ hour. They were bombed out of it again shortly afterwards. They had made the assault from Y7 & the O.C. 8th R.B. asked me to open fire on this point but was unable to do so for reasons stated above. Fired 8 rounds at BELLEWAARDE FARM searching for enemy trench mortar which had ~~done~~ done some damage to our trenches causing several casualties. Seven of my rounds took effect on the trenches ~~around~~ about the farm but failed to locate the mortar. This evening, during the usual bombardment of our support trenches with H.E., the enemy put over five 42 c.m's.	
	6.7.15		Fired 3 rounds at RAILWAY WOOD redoubt all taking effect. Came out of action	
C.R.A.	7.7.15 to 12.7.15		Out of action.	[initials] 23/7/15

1875 Wt. W593/826 1,000,000 4/15 J.B.C. & A. A.D.S.S./Forms/C. 2118.

Instructions regarding War Diaries and Intelligence Summaries are contained in F. S. Regs., Part II. and the Staff Manual respectively. Title Pages will be prepared in manuscript.

WAR DIARY
or
~~INTELLIGENCE SUMMARY~~
(Erase heading not required.)

Army Form C. 2118

27th Trench H. Bty

Place	Date	Hour	Summary of Events and Information	Remarks and references to Appendices
	July 11th		Battery taken over from Capt Beerbohm RFA by Lieut G I Thomas R.H.A	
			A new emplacement dug to bear on trenches in front of BELLEWAARDE FME –	
		3 pm	2 guns + 3 beds in position – Rounds fired at above trenches + a parapet blown in –	
	July 12th	4 am	Bombs fired at Redoubt opposite sunken road with great effect, + German mortar silenced.	
			During the day a new emplacement dug to bear on above redoubt	
	July 13th	3 am 6 pm 12 pm	Retaliation rounds fired at both above targets in reply to Trench mortars. Effect good + resulted in cessation of German fire. One bomb appeared to blow up a dug out as timber was seen flying about.	X
			Rumours of an attack on Redoubt at I.12 a 3.5.5. but postponed – Oxford + Bucks relieved by the K.S.L.I.	
	July 14th July 15th		Retaliation + offensive bombs fired occasionally at all targets. Effect good + distinct. Change took place, [illegible] transferred to us –	

1875 Wt. W593/826 1,000,000 4/15 J.B.C. & A. A.D.S.S./Forms/C. 2118.

Instructions regarding War Diaries and Intelligence Summaries are contained in F. S. Regs., Part II. and the Staff Manual respectively. Title Pages will be prepared in manuscript.

WAR DIARY
or
~~INTELLIGENCE SUMMARY~~
(Erase heading not required.)

Army Form C. 2118

29th Trench H.By

Place	Date	Hour	Summary of Events and Information	Remarks and references to Appendices
	July. 16th.		Usual firing at all targets.	
			A new emplacement prepared to bomb redoubt at I. 18. a. 5. 9	
	July. 17th.		Usual firing at all targets.	
		7. pm.	3 heavy & 1 light bombs fired at I. 18. a. 5. 9 with great effect. Near point of redoubt hit twice with heavy bombs & demolished.	
	July. 18th.	11. Am.	Fired at trenches near BELLEWARDE FME.	
			(Listening post in front of I. 12. a. 3. 3½. bombed – a light bomb into the work itself landed in the middle of, & distinctly upset a tea party.	X
	19th.	6.30. Am.	German Trench gun silenced by immediate & effective retaliation].	
	20th.	11. Am.	I. 12. a. 3. 3½. bombed in retaliation to rifle grenades, & stops them.	
		3 pm.	Sap head by BELLEWARDE FME bombed with good effect.	X
		9. pm.	Heavy bomb fired at I. 12. a. 3. 3½ & a working party stopped.	

1875 Wt. W593/826 1,000,000 4/15 J.B.C. & A. A.D.S.S./Forms/C. 2118.

Instructions regarding War Diaries and Intelligence Summaries are contained in F. S. Regs., Part II. and the Staff Manual respectively. Title Pages will be prepared in manuscript.

WAR DIARY
or
~~INTELLIGENCE SUMMARY~~
(Erase heading not required.)

Army Form C. 2118

29th T. H. BTY.

Place	Date	Hour	Summary of Events and Information	Remarks and references to Appendices
	July 21st		Usual retaliation at all targets	
			Several bombs fired at Redoubt in I. 18 a.5.9.	
	22nd		Sector round the new crater in HOOGE taken over from 3rd DIVN.	
			2 Guns carried across from RAILWAY WOOD, and one got into action against	
		10.pm	enemy trenches E. of HOOGE CHATEAU.	
	23rd	4.pm.	Heavy enemy trench mortar with shell weighing about 120lbs opens fire on the	
			crater & neighbouring trenches. Enemy trenches registered on & fired at with heavy	
			bombs.	
		7.pm	Heavily shelled by big howitzer.	
	24th	4.30pm.	Duel with enemy howitzer. One gun used to shell trenches. enemy's gun shelled	
			with the other one. It appears to be near I 18 b 8.6.	
		11.pm	One heavy bomb fired in retaliation.	
	25th	7.Am	Heavy duel again. Another enemy gun also firing from direction of BELLEWARDE	
			LAKE. No 2 gun knocked out & smashed. No. 1 gun buried. but general effect	No. 55119. Gnr Bradbury
			of our fire good, as it draws that of the enemy off the trenches.	killed.

1875 Wt. W593/826 1,000,000 4/15 J.B.C. & A. A.D.S.S./Forms/C. 2118.

Instructions regarding War Diaries and Intelligence Summaries are contained in F. S. Regs., Part II. and the Staff Manual respectively. Title Pages will be prepared in manuscript.

WAR DIARY
or
INTELLIGENCE SUMMARY
(Erase heading not required.)

Army Form C. 2118

29th T. H. BTY.

Place	Date	Hour	Summary of Events and Information	Remarks and references to Appendices
	July. 26th.		A new position made for No. 1. gun. Lt. Johnstone & 39th T. H. Bty take over RAILWAY WOOD sector.	
		8.30. pm.	A few heavy bombs fired in retaliation at new German Trench opposite the Crater.	21388 Gnr. Couchman 21181 Gnr Bates evacuated with nervous breakdown.
			The Bomb dug out near new gun position blown in.	
			Enemy search for our position with howitzers.	
	27th.	5 Am	Enemy mortar fires at 5 Am - but an aeroplane, flying low, makes retaliation impossible.	
		7 Am.	Several heavy bombs fired in further retaliation. 2 new guns brought up.	
			Arrangements made for O.C.s. 29th & 39th to work in relief at HOOGE.	

[signature] 2/8/15

1875 Wt. W593/826 1,000,000 4/15 J.B.C. & A. A.D.S.S./Forms/C. 2118.

Instructions regarding War Diaries and Intelligence Summaries are contained in F. S. Regs., Part II. and the Staff Manual respectively. Title Pages will be prepared in manuscript.

WAR DIARY
or
INTELLIGENCE SUMMARY
(Erase heading not required.)

Army Form C. 2118

Place	Date	Hour	Summary of Events and Information	Remarks and references to Appendices

1875 Wt. W593/826 1,000,000 4/15 J.B.C. & A. A.D.S.S./Forms/C. 2118.

Instructions regarding War Diaries and Intelligence Summaries are contained in F. S. Regs., Part II. and the Staff Manual respectively. Title Pages will be prepared in manuscript.

WAR DIARY
or
~~INTELLIGENCE~~ SUMMARY
(Erase heading not required.)

Army Form C. 2118

29th T.H. Bty.

Place	Date	Hour	Summary of Events and Information	Remarks and references to Appendices
	Aug 6th	8.00 a.m.	Received orders to report to 9th Inf. Bde H.Q. & to go into action	
		10.0 a.m.	Positions reconnoitred; one near CRUMP FARM, & one in trench A1 on north side of railway. Guns to occupy positions by night.	
		6.30 p.m.	Received orders only to occupy position in trench A1	
		10 p.m.	Took two guns up to the ~~trenches~~ with the R Scots Fusiliers. Lt. Clarkson R.G.A. joined the battery	
	Aug 7th.	8 a.m.	Dug emplacement to fire on the German barricade on the railway	
		2 p.m.	According to instructions received from 9th Inf. Bde. reconnoitred for position near CRUMPFARM, ~~to~~ to fire on new German works, but as yet the infantry know nothing of these works.	
	Aug 8th.	8.0 p.m.	Fired several rounds at the barricade & German trenches in retaliation	
		11 am	Retaliation on the German trenches with apparently good effect, as the German fire ceased.	
		4 p.m.	Dug new emplacement to bear on the German redoubt	
		8.0 p.m.	Fired at German redoubt.	
	Aug 9th	2.45 a.m.	Fired a good many rounds at the railway barricade, & the German redoubt	
		6 p.m.		
		10 a.m.	Fired again at the redoubt. 10 a.m. R. Scots Fusiliers relieved by Royal Fusiliers	

[initials] 26/8

1875 Wt. W593/826 1,000,000 4/15 J.B.C. & A. A.D.S.S./Forms/C. 2118.

Instructions regarding War Diaries and Intelligence Summaries are contained in F. S. Regs., Part II. and the Staff Manual respectively. Title Pages will be prepared in manuscript.

WAR DIARY
or
INTELLIGENCE SUMMARY
(Erase heading not required.)

Army Form C. 2118

Place	Date	Hour	Summary of Events and Information	Remarks and references to Appendices
	[illegible]	[illegible]	[illegible] instructions from Infantry [illegible]	
	[illegible]	[illegible]	[illegible]	

1875 Wt. W593/826 1,000,000 4/15 J.B.C. & A. A.D.S.S./Forms/C. 2118.

Army Form C. 2118

29th T.H.B. 29th T/Hwl/B.

Instructions regarding War Diaries and Intelligence Summaries are contained in F. S. Regs., Part II. and the Staff Manual respectively. Title Pages will be prepared in manuscript.

WAR DIARY
or
~~INTELLIGENCE SUMMARY~~
(Erase heading not required.)

Place	Date	Hour	Summary of Events and Information	Remarks and references to Appendices
	17th	8.30am.	Fired in retaliation to enemy mortar	
		12 midy	Fired in retaliation to enemy mortar. 1 'Minenwerfer' was fired but did no damage.	
		6.0pm	Fired at new German work on north side of railway. Parapet hit.	
			Three bombs fired today failed to burst, & one burst in air.	
	18th	12 mid.	Got Field Arty to Silence Enemy's "Minenwerfer".	
	19th		1 Pte Carmelling (Strapped) } Sent to dressing Station.	
	20th		1 Pte Dislocated Knee. }	
	21/22nd		all quiet.	

1875 Wt. W593/826 1,000,000 4/15 J.B.C. & A. A.D.S.S./Forms/C. 2118.

Instructions regarding War Diaries and Intelligence Summaries are contained in F. S. Regs., Part II. and the Staff Manual respectively. Title Pages will be prepared in manuscript.

WAR DIARY
or
INTELLIGENCE SUMMARY
(Erase heading not required.)

Army Form C. 2118

Place	Date	Hour	Summary of Events and Information	Remarks and references to Appendices

1875 Wt. W593/826 1,000,000 4/15 J.B.C. & A. A.D.S.S./Forms/C. 2118.

Instructions regarding War Diaries and Intelligence Summaries are contained in F. S. Regs., Part II. and the Staff Manual respectively. Title Pages will be prepared in manuscript.

WAR DIARY
or
INTELLIGENCE SUMMARY
(Erase heading not required.)

Army Form C. 2118

Place	Date	Hour	Summary of Events and Information	Remarks and references to Appendices
	Sept 2nd	5am	Fired three large bombs at BARRIER with good effect.	
		5.30am	Fired four large bombs at REDOUBT two failed to burst the other two did great damage. In both cases fired in retaliation to German mortars, which quietened down.	
		about 10pm	K.O.Y.L.I relieved by Durham L.I.	
	3rd	–	Situation quiet, except for artillery bombardment towards RAILWAY WOOD & HOOGE. Sgt C Higgins relieved by Capt Firth W R Regt. C Higgins Sgt	
	4th	noon	Registered a new machine gun emplacement with No1 gun. Fired 6 Leonies. Altered position of No1 gun about 10 degrees to left.	
	5th		Too wet to do anything but attempt to keep ammunition etc dry & bale out.	
	6th	noon	Fired 6 Leonies on [illegible] point just S. of Railway Line. Two with good effect. Remainder of T tubes failed to fire owing to wet.	
		9-15pm	Fired 1 Light from No 2 [illegible] (Two Islands) with very good effect on Enemy's trenches S. of Railway Line.	
	7th	noon	Fired 1 Heavy & 6 Light (Two Islands) with very good effect on Enemy's fire trench. One Dud landed on parapet of Enemy's fire trench.	
	–	–	Arranged Routine orders for Relief in action & improved dug-outs.	
	Sanctuary 7th	7.45pm	Handed over my Battery to Lieut. Clarkson on Relief.	

29 Trench Mortar Bty
Sheet to complete Vol I
Jan
Vol

29th Trench Mortar Bty

Army Form C. 2118.

WAR DIARY
or
~~INTELLIGENCE SUMMARY.~~
(Erase heading not required.)

Instructions regarding War Diaries and Intelligence Summaries are contained in F. S. Regs., Part II. and the Staff Manual respectively. Title pages will be prepared in manuscript.

Place	Date	Hour	Summary of Events and Information	Remarks and references to Appendices
Trenches Sanctuary Wood	7/1/16	5.30 P.M.	Took over Battery.	
	8/1/16		Selected gun positions for the 2 inch + 4 inch guns. Completed bomb store in Maple Copse.	
	9/1/16		Fired 11 rounds from 4 inch gun from B2, at the "Birdcage" + the communication trench leading to it. This is a work about 25 yds from our trenches + is used by the enemy as an observation + bombing post. The first round was a "dud" + the second struck a tree just in front of the target, breaking off the fuze. Five rounds were direct hits on the "Birdcage" + exploded with excellent effect, the woodwork being completely destroyed. Two shells landed in the communication trench damaging the parapet + two were just over the target. The result of the shoot was good as the "Birdcage" was badly damaged. The shoot was interesting, also as the task was rather beyond the scope of so light a shell, + it was only the fact of the shells landing right in the "Birdcage" that caused its demolition	
	10/1/16		Commenced building position for 2 inch gun.	
		1 P.M.	I was relieved by 2/Lt A Hutchison.	

29th Trench Mortar Battery
[signature] 2/Lt

Y50 Trench Motar Bty
late 29 TM Bty

Vol III

502

Army Form C. 2118.

Instructions regarding War Diaries and Intelligence Summaries are contained in F. S. Regs., Part II. and the Staff Manual respectively. Title pages will be prepared in manuscript.

WAR DIARY or ~~INTELLIGENCE SUMMARY~~. of Y.50 Trench Mortar Battery

(Erase heading not required.)

Place	Date	Hour	Summary of Events and Information	Remarks and references to Appendices
F 22 Central	1st – 5th		These days were spent in billets when the usual work was carried through. Physical Drill. Squad Drill and Semaphore.	

T2134. Wt. W708—776. 500000. 4/15. Sir J. C. & S.

Instructions regarding War Diaries and Intelligence Summaries are contained in F. S. Regs., Part II. and the Staff Manual respectively. Title pages will be prepared in manuscript.

WAR DIARY
or
~~INTELLIGENCE SUMMARY.~~

(Erase heading not required.)

Of Y.50 Trench Mortar Battery.

Army Form C. 2118.

Place	Date	Hour	Summary of Events and Information	Remarks and references to Appendices
	March			
I 30 a 8.4	6th		Detachment under Lt L B Walker relieved by detachment under Lt R Macleod. Cleaned up all guns and sorted out bomb stores. Finished revetting of X (left) gun. Reported to C.O 7th R.F. who said that he wanted quietness to repair trenches.	
	7th		Fired 8 rounds from Right 1½ ins gun on points between I 30 c.5.4 and c 3.7. Revetted back of 2" emplacement. Owing to abnormal fall of rain all 1½" gun pits required draining. This was done. Continued 2" sap and began bomb store in sap.	
	8th		Continued 2" sap and bomb store. Began dug-out for men. Relief takes place 7th R F relieved by 6th R.F.	
	9th		Met O C at Brigade H.Q. Told to put 2 ins in position to fire on I 29 d 8.7 (Hun snout). Cleared out old 2" position and laid down timber. Continued new 2 ins position. Sent 2" piece to X Battery.	
	10th		Conference with C O 7th R F and arranged strafe. Continued work on 2"	

T2134. Wt. W708–776. 500000. 4/15. Sir J. C. & S.

Instructions regarding War Diaries and Intelligence Summaries are contained in F. S. Regs., Part II. and the Staff Manual respectively. Title pages will be prepared in manuscript.

WAR DIARY ~~or~~ ~~INTELLIGENCE SUMMARY~~. of Y.50 Trench Mortar Battery.

(*Erase heading not required.*)

Army Form C. 2118.

Place	Date	Hour	Summary of Events and Information	Remarks and references to Appendices
I 30 a 8.4	10th	4.30pm	Fired 4 rounds 1½" from Y (right) gun to register for shoot.	
			Fired 10 rounds 3.7 in retaliation for 'sausages' Got 2" piece from H.Q.	
	11th		Continued work on sap and timbered same.	
		6.30pm	Had a half hour shoot. Fired 24 rounds 1½" on enemy trenches between I 30 c 5.7 and c 3.7. Fired 14 rounds 2 ins on M.G. emplacement at I 30 c 5.7	
		7.30pm to 9pm	Fired 38 rounds 3.7 in retaliation for 'sausages' sent over.	
	12th		Observed damage done previous night. Found that emplacement had been hit 3 times, none doing very complete damage.	
			One 1½" apparently fell on top of M.G emplacement and failed to penetrate. Found that 4.2 in shell had damaged entrance to 2" sap. Spent morning repairing. Cleaned all guns and stores	
	13th		Continued 2" position Began cleaning up ready for relief.	

T2134. Wt. W708-776. 500000. 4/15. Sir J. C. & S.

Instructions regarding War Diaries and Intelligence Summaries are contained in F. S. Regs., Part II. and the Staff Manual respectively. Title pages will be prepared in manuscript.

WAR DIARY
or
~~INTELLIGENCE~~ SUMMARY.
(Erase heading not required.)

of Y.50 Trench Mortar Battery

Army Form C. 2118.

Place	Date	Hour	Summary of Events and Information	Remarks and references to Appendices
I 30 c x 4	13th		Detachment under Lt Macleod relieved by detachment under Lt Macnamara. Reported to O C 7th [illegible].	
	14th		Brought bombs from central bomb store. To 2 [illegible] gun [illegible] 2 gun owing to it being in bad ground. Began digging at C Trench about [illegible] yards long then emplacement to be made	
	15th		Continued work on 2" sap and bomb store. Continued work on trench at 2 gun position and sandbagged. No firing allowed owing to repairs to breastworks	
	16th		Finished trench and began emplacement for 2 gun. Dug out emplacement and [illegible] down bed of timber. Put in 12" bed and gun.	
	17th		Asked by O C to have gun to fire on front. [illegible] up bed of two [illegible] and [illegible] so as to be able to fire on point wanted.	
	18th		Continued digging at 2" emplacement.	

T2131. Wt. W708—776. 500000. 4/15. Sir J. C. & S.

Instructions regarding War Diaries and Intelligence Summaries are contained in F. S. Regs., Part II. and the Staff Manual respectively. Title pages will be prepared in manuscript.

WAR DIARY or ~~INTELLIGENCE SUMMARY~~. of Y.50 Trench Mortar Battery.

(Erase heading not required.)

Army Form C. 2118.

Place	Date	Hour	Summary of Events and Information	Remarks and references to Appendices
I 30 9 8.4	19th		Continued work on 2" sap. Work during day was hindered owing to lack of wood.	
	20th		Detachment under Lt Macnamara relieved by detachment under Lt R Macleod. Reported to O C 5th Yorks who said he wished quietness to repair trenches damaged that morning. Sent 1½" gun to X battery. Bomb store in sap worked on.	
	21st		Repaired X gun emplacement damaged by shell fire. Drained C.T leading to emplacement. Continued work on 2" sap.	
	22nd		Repaired bomb store at X gun. Brought bombs to Z gun. Continued 2" sap.	
	23rd		Completed bomb store in sap and began work on dug-out. Work hampered owing to lack of wood. Put down 2" bed in new position in sap.	
	24th		Continued work on dug-out in sap and put in shelves etc for fuzes and charges	

T2134. Wt. W708–776. 500000. 4/15. Sir J. C. & S.

Instructions regarding War Diaries and Intelligence Summaries are contained in F. S. Regs., Part II. and the Staff Manual respectively. Title pages will be prepared in manuscript.

WAR DIARY ~~or INTELLIGENCE SUMMARY~~ of Y.50 Trench Mortar Battery

(*Erase heading not required.*)

Army Form C. 2118.

Place	Date	Hour	Summary of Events and Information	Remarks and references to Appendices
T 30 [illegible]	25th		Brought 2" gun piece to new sap also bombs fuzes etc. Drained 2 gun position and cleaned it out. Laid down bed [illegible]. Sent 2 [illegible] 12" beds back to billets	
	26th		[illegible] clean up [illegible] [illegible] had been damaged by shell fire.	
	27th		[illegible]	
	28th		[illegible] spent in clearing up. Took out X gun and bed and put in new one for Canadians. Sent 2 1/2" guns to dump to be brought to billets	
	29th		Fired 3 rounds from 2" in new sap in order to register. Continued clearing up. Wire from OC says "Relieved by Canadians tomorrow". Took both 2" beds out and cleaned emplacement.	

T2131. Wt. W708–776. 500000. 4/15. Sir J. C. & S.

Instructions regarding War Diaries and Intelligence Summaries are contained in F. S. Regs., Part II. and the Staff Manual respectively. Title pages will be prepared in manuscript.

WAR DIARY of Y.50 Trench Mortar Battery.

or

~~INTELLIGENCE SUMMARY~~.

(Erase heading not required.)

Army Form C. 2118.

Place	Date	Hour	Summary of Events and Information	Remarks and references to Appendices
I 30 a 8.4	30th		Handed over all Stores and ammunition to X 1 C Battery who relieved. Detachment were under Sergt Halliday.	
	31st		Battery moved from old area to M 24 central	
			R. Macleod Lieut	

T2134. Wt. W708—776. 500000. 4/15. Sir J. C. & S.

- 1 -

Z 50 TM Blt

~~IV~~ I

Vol ~~IV~~ I

Army Form C. 2118.

Instructions regarding War Diaries and Intelligence Summaries are contained in F. S. Regs., Part II. and the Staff Manual respectively. Title Pages will be prepared in manuscript.

WAR DIARY ~~or INTELLIGENCE~~ SUMMARY of Z 50 T. M. Battery

(Erase heading not required.)

Place	Date	Hour	Summary of Events and Information	Remarks and references to Appendices
N18C	APRIL 2		4 1½ guns and beds. 4 permanent beds. 2 tool boxes and 2 telephones brought up to new area and left in bomb store under N.C.O.	
	3		Lieut Bennet took over from X2C T.M. Battery. 2 guns being in Reserve positions in H5 and K1A by 9.30 p.m. Took over 82 heavy and 60 light 1½ bombs not complete.	
	4		Made careful survey of our trenches from H2 to K1 and chose new positions in CT between K1A and K1 and in Park Avenue. - working all day on reserve position in H5 and carrying up ammunition Enemy sent over rum-jars and sausages - retaliation impossible as no positions ready.	
	5		Put 1½ gun in J10 and fired 2 rounds from it at 7.30 p.m in retaliation Put guns in H5 and Park Avenue. Infantry party during day working on positions. Ammunition carried up in evening.	
	6	8.30 AM - 8 p.m	Infantry party at work on new positions and stores. Brought up 2 ins gun and Stokes. Fuzed and carried up Stokes ammunition to J10. Fired 12 rounds Stokes and 3 1½ at 3.30 p.m silencing	

2449 Wt. W14957/M90 750,000 1/16 J.B.C. & A. Forms/C.2118/12.

Instructions regarding War Diaries and Intelligence Summaries are contained in F. S. Regs., Part II. and the Staff Manual respectively. Title Pages will be prepared in manuscript.

WAR DIARY

or

~~INTELLIGENCE~~ SUMMARY

(Erase heading not required.)

of Z 50 T.M. Battery

Army Form C. 2118.

Place	Date	Hour	Summary of Events and Information	Remarks and references to Appendices
			enemy [illegible] ammunition at night.	
	7		Made preparations for an hours strafe and had men standing by all day. Strafe took place from [illegible] 40 rounds fired on enemy wire and trenches I24a20 to I24a78. Parapet breached in several places. Enemy retaliated with whizz-bangs three times during day [illegible] grenades and [illegible] [illegible] Continued work on 2 emplacements [illegible]	
	8		[illegible]	
	9		[illegible]	

Instructions regarding War Diaries and Intelligence Summaries are contained in F. S. Regs., Part II. and the Staff Manual respectively. Title Pages will be prepared in manuscript.

WAR DIARY or ~~INTELLIGENCE~~ SUMMARY of Z 50 T.M. Battery

(Erase heading not required.)

Army Form C. 2118.

Place	Date	Hour	Summary of Events and Information	Remarks and references to Appendices
N18 C	10		Began bombstore at 1½" gun to right of K.A. Built bomb store at Park Avenue and roofed it. During night sand-bagged top and sides of bomb store and brought up frames for bomb store at H5.	
	11		Put in frame work of bomb store and roofed same. By night sand bagged position. Made a C.T. from Park Avenue to bomb store and gun in wood near Park Avenue. Sandbagged gun emplacement. Removed Stokes gun from K.A and brought it to central bomb store, in order to hand it over to Light Battery. Cleaned up all guns. Owing to very heavy shelling work was hindered.	
	12		Cleaned up central bomb store and finished C.T. to Park Avenue gun. Put gun bed in and brought 2" bombs from bomb store. Very heavy shelling during afternoon. Bomb store and gun emplacement at H5 completely wrecked also 2" position in K.A.	

2449 Wt. W14957/M90 750,000 1/16 J.B.C. & A. Forms/C.2118/12.

Instructions regarding War Diaries and Intelligence Summaries are contained in F. S. Regs., Part II. and the Staff Manual respectively. Title Pages will be prepared in manuscript.

WAR DIARY
or
~~INTELLIGENCE SUMMARY~~

(Erase heading not required.)

Army Form C. 2118.

Place	Date	Hour	Summary of Events and Information	Remarks and references to Appendices
[illegible]	13		[illegible] ... in Park Avenue ... [illegible] ... 8th N.F. relieved by 4th N.F.	
	14		[illegible] gun from [illegible] damaged and [illegible] Park Avenue.	
	[illegible]		[illegible]	
		[illegible]	[illegible] ... Park [illegible]	

2449 Wt. W14957/M90 750,000 1/16 J.B.C. & A. Forms/C.2118/12.

Army Form C. 2118.

Instructions regarding War Diaries and Intelligence Summaries are contained in F. S. Regs., Part II. and the Staff Manual respectively. Title Pages will be prepared in manuscript.

WAR DIARY or ~~INTELLIGENCE~~ SUMMARY

of 250 T.M. Battery.

(Erase heading not required.)

Place	Date	Hour	Summary of Events and Information	Remarks and references to Appendices
N 18 C	15		between N24 b 1.2 and N24 a 7.6, also registered on C T N24 b 0.5	
		6 pm	Fired 8 rounds from 1½ gun in J 10 in retaliation for sausages sent over. also fired 4 rounds from 1½" in J 3 5. Enemy mortars were silenced.	
	16		Repaired 1½" emplacement at N24 a 2.5 which had again been damaged by shell fire; drained position. Repaired entrance to temporary bomb store in J 3 5 Cleaned up all guns and stores.	
		4.30 pm	Fired 22 rounds from 1½ in J 3 5 on points in enemy lines between N24 a 7.6 and a 7.9. Fired 10 rounds from 1½ in J 10. Fired 3 rounds from 2" in Park Avenue. The fourth round (an Ammonal bomb) burst in the muzzle of the gun killing the Corporal in charge and wounding a Gunner.	
		8 pm	Carried ammunition from dump to central bomb store.	

2449 Wt. W14957/M90 750,000 1/16 J.B.C. & A. Forms/C.2118/12.

WAR DIARY
or
~~INTELLIGENCE~~ SUMMARY
(Erase heading not required.)

of Z 50 T M Battery

Army Form C. 2118.

Instructions regarding War Diaries and Intelligence Summaries are contained in F. S. Regs., Part II. and the Staff Manual respectively. Title Pages will be prepared in manuscript.

Place	Date	Hour	Summary of Events and Information	Remarks and references to Appendices
Y 18 c	17		Detachment under Lieut R. MacLeod relieved by detachment under Lieut Hutchison.	
		2 pm	Lieut Hutchison recalled to T.M. Head quarters. Sgt Howlett in charge. Owing to heavy shelling no work possible	
	18		Attempted to drain position in [illegible] but could not do so owing to gun emplacement being lower than trench. Cleared up bomb store and [illegible] guns. Returned damaged 2" gun and [illegible] to H.Q.	
			[illegible] working in bomb store in T 3. Cleaned out stores.	
			[illegible] shelled and in getting to cover one gunner was accidently wounded	
			Fired [illegible] rounds from 2" gun in T 10 in retaliation for "sausages"	
	20		[illegible] on bomb store in T 3. Gun taken out of emplacement as it was full of water. Drained position.	
		7 pm	Fired five rounds from gun in T 10 in retaliation. Brought up ammunition from dump to central bomb store.	
	21	8 am	Fired 7 rounds from gun in T 10 in retaliation for sausages	
			Heavily shelled during day with the result that gun emplacement	

2449 Wt. W14957/M90 750,000 1/16 J.B.C. & A. Forms/C.2118/12.

Army Form C. 2118.

Instructions regarding War Diaries and Intelligence Summaries are contained in F. S. Regs., Part II. and the Staff Manual respectively. Title Pages will be prepared in manuscript.

WAR DIARY or ~~INTELLIGENCE SUMMARY~~ of Z 50 T.M. Battery.

(Erase heading not required.)

Place	Date	Hour	Summary of Events and Information	Remarks and references to Appendices
N 18 C			in J 35 was destroyed and gun buried.	
	22		Spent most part of day digging out 1½" gun and attempting to repair emplacement. Fired 6 rounds from gun in J 10 in retaliation for sausages.	
	23	8 A.M.	Fired 4 rounds from J 10.	
		3 P.M.	Detachment under Lt R Macleod relieved detachment under Sgt Howlett. Repaired 2" position in Park Avenue and carried bombs to bomb store at gun. Cleaned all guns and stores.	
	24		Removed 1½" gun from J 10. Cleaned out position and put new gun platform in. Put in 2" gun and bed.	
		2 p.m	Fired 5 rounds 2" from Park Avenue on enemy trenches round Petit Bois (N 24 a 7.6).	
		4 p.m	Fired 9 rounds 2" on same points; both in retaliation for sausages and "rum jars". Repaired 1½" gun position in J 35 and had gun laid to fire on mine crater opposite K 1.	

2449 Wt. W14957/M90 750,000 1/16 J.B.C. & A. Forms/C.2118/12.

Instructions regarding War Diaries and Intelligence Summaries are contained in F. S. Regs., Part II. and the Staff Manual respectively. Title Pages will be prepared in manuscript.

WAR DIARY
or
~~INTELLIGENCE~~ SUMMARY of Z 50 T M Battery.
(Erase heading not required.)

Army Form C. 2118.

Place	Date	Hour	Summary of Events and Information	Remarks and references to Appendices
A 18 C	23		O. C.'s 2" position behind J 4 which previously had been overlooked was drained and left to dry. This position requires a good deal of work but will make a good emplacement.	
		3 pm	Took out 1½" gun in SP 13. Fired 10 rounds of 2" from gun in Park Avenue. Brought 20 rounds from central bomb store to this gun.	
		8 pm	Sent 3 1½" gun pieces and 2 bed to billets, as all 1½ guns were recalled.	
A 18 C	2[illegible]	8 am.	Continued work on gun position behind J 4. Made new 2" emplacement	
		4 pm	behind H 3 and put in 2" bed. Sent to billets all 1½" ammunition	
		6 pm	in possession. Brought up 2 ins ammunition from dump. Central bomb store was partially destroyed by a direct hit from 5.9	
	24	1 am.	Fired 6 rounds from 2" in retaliation for Sausages — took 1½" gun and bed out of J 30 and 1½" bed out of K 10. Both were sent to billets with remainder of stores.	
		4 pm	Fired 9 rounds 2" from gun in Park Avenue in retaliation for Sausages.	

2449 Wt. W14957/M90 750,000 1/16 J.B.C. & A. Forms/C.2118/12.

Army Form C. 2118.

Instructions regarding War Diaries and Intelligence Summaries are contained in F. S. Regs., Part II. and the Staff Manual respectively. Title Pages will be prepared in manuscript.

WAR DIARY or ~~INTELLIGENCE SUMMARY~~ of Z 50 T M. Battery

(Erase heading not required.)

Place	Date	Hour	Summary of Events and Information	Remarks and references to Appendices
N 18 C	27	7 p.m	Began taking down bomb store destroyed by shell fire.	
	28		Continued work on central bomb store. Obtained 2 new pieces for steel roof. Two ins position behind J 4 destroyed by shell fire. New position now necessary	
		6 A.M	Fired 7 rounds from 2" on points in enemy line in Petit Bois.	
		10 A.M	Repaired 2" position in J 10 also bomb store and gun bed in Park Avenue. Fired 5 rounds between 2 p.m and 6 p.m in retaliation for sausages and rum jars. Carried ammunition from dump to bomb store in P. avenue.	
	29	5 A.M.	Fired 2 rounds from 2" in retaliation. Continued work on central bombstore which is now practically completed. Made small bombstore in H3. Fired 5 rounds 2" on points between N 24 a 7.6 and a 7.9. Considerable damage was done.	
		8 p.m	Carried 30 rounds 2" from dump to central bomb store.	

2449 Wt. W14957/M90 750,000 1/16 J.B.C. & A. Forms/C.2118/12.

Army Form C. 2118.

Instructions regarding War Diaries and Intelligence Summaries are contained in F. S. Regs., Part II. and the Staff Manual respectively. Title Pages will be prepared in manuscript.

WAR DIARY

or

~~INTELLIGENCE SUMMARY~~

(Erase heading not required.)

Z 30 T.M. Battery

Place	Date	Hour	Summary of Events and Information	Remarks and references to Appendices
N 15 c	30	am	Fired 10 rounds 2" at enemy trenches 12 a 7.6	
			Spent morning cleaning up [illegible] store and guns for relief.	
			Finished central [illegible]	
		3pm	Fired 12 rounds 2" on points between 12 a 7.6 and a 7.9	
			Considerable damage done.	
		4pm	Relieved by Z 30 T.M. Battery to whom I handed over guns and [illegible]	

R. Rac[illegible] Lt

O.C. Z 30 T.M. By

2449 Wt. W14957/M90 750,000 1/16 J.B.C. & A. Forms/C.2118/12.

Instructions regarding War Diaries and Intelligence Summaries are contained in F. S. Regs., Part II. and the Staff Manual respectively. Title pages will be prepared in manuscript.

Army Form C. 2118.

WAR DIARY
or
~~INTELLIGENCE SUMMARY~~.
(Erase heading not required.)

of Z 50 Trench Mortar Battery

Vol 2

Place	Date	Hour	Summary of Events and Information	Remarks and references to Appendices
	MAY			
Q.28.d.1.7	1	9 AM	Battery proceeded to Ecche for rest.	
	2	6.30 -12.30	Training. Route March. 2" Mortar Instruction. Semaphore Gun Drill	
	3	..	Training. Gun Drill. Telephony Preparing 2" gun emplacement.	
	4	..	Training. Preparing 2" emplacement. Gun Drill. Telephony.	
	5	..	Telephony. Gun Drill.	
	6	..	Fatigues. (Moving to new camp)	
	7	10 AM	Rifle Inspection.	
		11.30.	Church Parade.	
	8	....	Training 2" Gun drill. Telephony. 2" Gun Instruction.	
	9	....	Training 2" Gun drill. Semaphore. Instruction in bombs and fuzes.	
	10	....	Training. Instruction in D.A. fuze. Squad Drill. Semaphore.	
	11	....	Training 2" Gun Drill. Telephony. Squad Drill with rifles.	
	12	....	Training Preparing 2" Gun emplacement.	
	13	....	Training Musketry. Gun Drill. Telephony	
	14	10 A.M.	Church Parade. Rifle Inspection.	

T2134. Wt. W708—776. 500000. 4/15. Sir J. C. & S.

Instructions regarding War Diaries and Intelligence Summaries are contained in F. S. Regs., Part II. and the Staff Manual respectively. Title pages will be prepared in manuscript.

WAR DIARY
or
~~INTELLIGENCE SUMMARY.~~
(Erase heading not required.)

Army Form C. 2118.

250 T M Battery

Place	Date	Hour	Summary of Events and Information	Remarks and references to Appendices
Q 28 d 1.1	15	[illegible]	[illegible] gun Drill. Musketry. Tube Helmet Drill.	
	16	"	Training Telephony. 2" Gun Drill. Tube Helmet Drill	
	17	"	[illegible] Musketry. gun Drill.	
	18	"	[illegible] Drill. [illegible] gun Drill.	
	19	"	[illegible] Telephony. Gun Drill.	
	20	"	[illegible] Drill. [illegible] gun Drill.	
	[illegible]	10 A.M.	Church Parade.	
	22	[illegible]	[illegible]	
	23		[illegible]	
	24		[illegible]	
	25		[illegible]	
	26		250 [illegible] Battery [illegible] 250 [illegible] 3 guns	
			in action. Placed 2 men on guns in [illegible]	
			H2 [illegible]	
	27	[illegible] A.M.	[illegible] All quiet.	
		2.30 P.M.	Fired 12 rounds from gun in L3 and [illegible] rounds from gun in	

T2134. Wt. W708–776. 500000. 4/15. Sir J. C. & S.

Army Form C. 2118.

Instructions regarding War Diaries and Intelligence Summaries are contained in F. S. Regs., Part II. and the Staff Manual respectively. Title pages will be prepared in manuscript.

WAR DIARY
or
INTELLIGENCE SUMMARY.
(Erase heading not required.)

of 250 T.M. Battery

Place	Date	Hour	Summary of Events and Information	Remarks and references to Appendices
~~[illegible]~~ Sheet 28 N 18 C	27	2 P.M.	Park Avenue. After this enemy was quiet. Dug out in Park Avenue slightly damaged. Repaired it.	
		8.30 PM.	Had an infantry working party of 20 men to carry ammunition.	
	28	2 A.M.	Fired 7 rounds from Park Avenue and 9 rounds from L3 after this all was quiet.	
		2 P.M.	Fired 40 rounds into Petit Bois and CT running through same.	
		7.30 PM	Had working party of 20 men to carry up ammunition.	
	29.	2 AM	Stood to for 2 hours. Fired 13 rounds from Park Avenue & L3 into Crater & Petit Bois.	
		4 P.M.	Registered 4 rounds on crater from gun in K1. Park avenue and L3 fired in retaliation and both were praised by officers observing.	
		8 PM.	Had working party to bring up bombs.	
		12.30 AM	Organised straf fired 15 rounds from K1 & Park Avenue on Crater.	

Instructions regarding War Diaries and Intelligence Summaries are contained in F. S. Regs., Part II. and the Staff Manual respectively. Title pages will be prepared in manuscript.

WAR DIARY
or
~~INTELLIGENCE SUMMARY.~~
(Erase heading not required.)

Army Form C. 2118.

Y 2 50 T M Battery

Place	Date	Hour	Summary of Events and Information	Remarks and references to Appendices
	30.	2 PM	Registered gun in Park Avenue on Crater.	
		10 PM	Fired 9 rounds on N Crater. Had to cease fire owing to heavy shell fire by crumps and minnies.	
	31	10 AM	Cleaned all guns and stores.	
		2 PM	Strafe in retaliation 24 rounds fired on Petit Bois by the gun and Park Avenue. Heavily shelled. Direct hit on L3 gun wounding one man. Gun not damaged.	
		9 PM	Ammunition party of 20 men to carry [illegible].	

R. Maclean [illegible]
OC Z 50 Bty

T2131. Wt. W708–776. 500000. 4/15. Sir J. C. & S.

Instructions regarding War Diaries and Intelligence Summaries are contained in F. S. Regs., Part II. and the Staff Manual respectively. Title Pages will be prepared in manuscript.

WAR DIARY
or
~~INTELLIGENCE SUMMARY~~
(Erase heading not required.)

of Z 50 T. M Battery

Army Form C. 2118.

Vol 3

Place	Date	Hour	Summary of Events and Information	Remarks and references to Appendices
	June			
N 17 D	1	9 AM	Went round all positions Repaired emplacements and had working party on K.A positions.	
	2	8 pm	Working party for ammunition.	
		9 AM	Went round all guns.	
		3 pm	Fired 60 rounds in front line and Crater N 18 C 8 0 50 rounds of ammunition and 3 guns brought up at night.	
	3		Visited all guns. Repaired position in Park Avenue Worked on guns all day.	
	4	12.30 AM	Very heavy shelling Enemy fired rum jars and sausages. Retaliated firing 12 rounds from H_2 and 9 from L3.	
		9 AM.	Got all guns in order for relief. Work on all positions.	
	5		Detachment under Lt Macleod relieved detachment under 2 Lt Corder. Visited Brigade Headquarters for Conference. Put 2 guns in position in Park Avenue, and brought bombs to bomb store there.	

Instructions regarding War Diaries and Intelligence Summaries are contained in F. S. Regs., Part II. and the Staff Manual respectively. Title Pages will be prepared in manuscript.

WAR DIARY
or
INTELLIGENCE SUMMARY
(Erase heading not required.)

Army Form C. 2118.

Place	Date	Hour	Summary of Events and Information	Remarks and references to Appendices

2449 Wt. W14957/M90 750,000 1/16 J.B.C. & A. Forms/C.2118/12.

Instructions regarding War Diaries and Intelligence Summaries are contained in F. S. Regs., Part II. and the Staff Manual respectively. Title Pages will be prepared in manuscript.

WAR DIARY ~~or~~ ~~INTELLIGENCE SUMMARY~~ of 250 T. M Battery

(*Erase heading not required.*)

Army Form C. 2118.

Place	Date	Hour	Summary of Events and Information	Remarks and references to Appendices
	June			
N 17 D	9	8 AM	Removed guns from S P. 13. Carried up ammunition to L 3 gun. Replenished all other bomb stores.	
		12 noon	Fired 4 rounds from gun in Park Avenue and 15 from gun in L3 in retaliation.	
			Recalled to H Q's Sgt Howlett takes charge.	
		2 to 6 pm	Fired 16 rounds on Crater in retaliation.	
	10		Work on all positions. Fired 10 rounds from gun in P. Avenue. 6 from gun in H 2.	
		9 pm	Carried up ammunition	
	11.	6 P.M	Fired 8 rounds from K.I.A. Work continued all day on positions.	
		9 PM	Carried up ammunition.	
	12	9.30 AM	Sgt Matthews relieved Sgt Howlett.	
		4.30 PM	In retaliation for sausages etc fired 25 rounds in old and new Craters doing some damage.	

2449 Wt. W14957/M90 750,000 1/16 J.B.C. & A. Forms/C.2118/12.

Army Form C. 2118.

Instructions regarding War Diaries and Intelligence Summaries are contained in F. S. Regs., Part II. and the Staff Manual respectively. Title Pages will be prepared in manuscript.

WAR DIARY
or
INTELLIGENCE SUMMARY

(Erase heading not required.)

Place	Date	Hour	Summary of Events and Information	Remarks and references to Appendices

2449 Wt. W14957/M90 750,000 1/16 J.B.C. & A. Forms/C.2118/12.

Instructions regarding War Diaries and Intelligence Summaries are contained in F. S. Regs., Part II. and the Staff Manual respectively. Title pages will be prepared in manuscript.

WAR DIARY ~~or INTELLIGENCE SUMMARY~~. of Z 50 T.M. Battery

(Erase heading not required.)

Army Form C. 2118.

Place	Date	Hour	Summary of Events and Information	Remarks and references to Appendices
June				
N1TD	18	430PM	Relief under Lt Macleod relieved Lt Cooler. Went round all guns and detailed men to clean up each one.	
	19		Sandbagged round L3 position. Began bombstore at KIA(R). Drained KIA left gun and relaid bed. Worked on Canadian drain. and Park Avenue Positions	
		9pm	Brought up ammunition	
		10pm	Fired 10 rounds from guns in Park Avenue and KIA on enemy crater and front line.	
	20	6AM	Fired 5 rounds from gun in KIA on enemy Crater. Continued work on bomb store in KIA.(R). (also on positions in L3 and Park Avenue.	
		4pm.	Fired 3 rounds from L3 in retaliation	
			Fired 7 rounds from gun in Park Avenue.	
		10pm	Carried up ammunition.	
	21		Fired 28 rounds from gun in Park Avenue & KIA. on enemy Crater.	

Instructions regarding War Diaries and Intelligence Summaries are contained in F. S. Regs., Part II. and the Staff Manual respectively. Title pages will be prepared in manuscript.

WAR DIARY

or

~~INTELLIGENCE SUMMARY.~~

(Erase heading not required.)

Army Form C. 2118.

Place	Date	Hour	Summary of Events and Information	Remarks and references to Appendices

T2134. Wt. W708–776. 500000. 4/15. Sir J. C. & S.

Instructions regarding War Diaries and Intelligence Summaries are contained in F. S. Regs., Part II. and the Staff Manual respectively. Title pages will be prepared in manuscript.

WAR DIARY of Z 50 T.M. Bty

~~or~~

~~INTELLIGENCE SUMMARY.~~

(Erase heading not required.)

Army Form C. 2118.

Place	Date	Hour	Summary of Events and Information	Remarks and references to Appendices
	June			
N I Y D	27	10 AM	Fired 17 rounds from Park Avenue into Crater, 30 from K I A	
		3PM	Fired 7 rounds from K I A.	
			Work carried on. Shelling very heavy	
	28.		During day fired 52 rounds from Park Avenue and 51 rounds from H2 on to enemy wire. No work owing to shelling.	
	29.		During day fired 63 rounds from K I A. 54 from Park Avenue and 18 from H2.	
	30	1030AM	Fired 15 rounds from K I A and P Avenue in retaliation.	
		2pm	Fired 20 rounds from K I A into enemy wire behind Crater.	
		3pm.	Fired 30 rounds from H2 into enemy wire in front of Petit Bois.	
			R Macleod Lieut O C Z 50 Trench Mortar Battery	

Instructions regarding War Diaries and Intelligence Summaries are contained in F. S. Regs., Part II. and the Staff Manual respectively. Title Pages will be prepared in manuscript.

Army Form C. 2118.

WAR DIARY
or
~~INTELLIGENCE SUMMARY~~ of V.50 Heavy Trench Mortar Bty

(Erase heading not required.)

June

Vol 1

Place	Date	Hour	Summary of Events and Information	Remarks and references to Appendices
N.24.d.10.5	1/7/16	6am–4pm	At work on bomb store, gun drill & telephony	
"	2nd	"	Gun drill, fatigues. 20 men at work in right sector.	
"	3rd	"	Gun drill, semaphore signalling & fatigues. 2nd Lieut Galloway reported for duty.	
"	4.	9–10.30	Kit & rifle inspection. 6 men to X, Y, & Z batteries for duty in the trenches. 2nd Lieut Wright reported for duty	
"	5.	9–12.30	Fatigues & baths.	
"	6.	10–4	Gun drill, fatigues, semaphore signalling.	
"	7.	"	Fatigues, gun drill, etc.	
"	8.	"	ditto	
"	9.	"	ditto	
"	10.	"	ditto	
"	11.	9–10.30	Kit & rifle inspection. 6 men to X, Y & Z batteries for duty in trenches	
"	12.	6–4	Fatigues & baths.	
"	13.	"	Fatigues, building bomb store	
"	14.	"	ditto	

2449 Wt. W14957/M90 750,000 1/16 J.B.C. & A. Forms/C.2118/12.

Army Form C. 2118.

Instructions regarding War Diaries and Intelligence Summaries are contained in F. S. Regs., Part II. and the Staff Manual respectively. Title Pages will be prepared in manuscript.

WAR DIARY
or
~~INTELLIGENCE SUMMARY~~ of V.56 Heavy Trench Mortar Bty

(Erase heading not required.)

Place	Date	Hour	Summary of Events and Information	Remarks and references to Appendices
	July 1916			
M24d 10.5	15.	6am	Route march, fatigues. Time advanced 60 minutes	
"	16.	"	Fatigues, 6 men detailed for work in centre sector.	
"	17.	"	ditto	
"	18.	9-10.30am	Kit & rifle inspection, Church parade, 10 men for Z battery, & 6 each for X & Y for duty in trenches.	
"	19.	"	Fatigues and baths.	
"	20.	"	Fatigues and semaphore.	
"	21	"	Building bomb store, fatigues etc	
"	22		ditto	
"	23		Tailing bombs, fatigues, etc	
"	24.	"	Fatigues, tailing bombs, & baths. Fired 38 rounds in straffe.	
"	25.	9am.	Kit & rifle inspection, divine service. V battery took over left sub	
		5-30pm	sector of centre from Z battery. 2nd Lieut Browne attached & proceeded to trenches with battery 6 men to X & Y batteries for duty in trenches	
N24a4.4 &	26	2-0pm	Fired 31 rounds & worked on positions. Fatigues at billets.	
N24a27	27.	3-0pm	" 40 rounds & ditto ditto	
N24a44		12 midnight	2nd Lieut Browne wounded.	

2449 Wt. W14957/M90 750,000 1/16 J.B.C. & A. Forms/C.2118/12.

Army Form C. 2118.

Instructions regarding War Diaries and Intelligence Summaries are contained in F. S. Regs., Part II. and the Staff Manual respectively. Title Pages will be prepared in manuscript.

WAR DIARY
or
~~INTELLIGENCE~~ SUMMARY

(Erase heading not required.)

Place	Date	Hour	Summary of Events and Information	Remarks and references to Appendices
			H. C. Macnamara	

2449 Wt. W14957/M90 750,000 1/16 J.B.C. & A. Forms/C.2118/12.

July 1916

CONFIDENTIAL 50

MAP SHEET 28. S.W. 2.

Army Form C. 2118.

Instructions regarding War Diaries and Intelligence Summaries are contained in F. S. Regs., Part II. and the Staff Manual respectively. Title pages will be prepared in manuscript.

WAR DIARY

~~or~~

~~INTELLIGENCE SUMMARY.~~

(Erase heading not required.)

Vol 12

50th Divl T.M. ~~Bgde~~ Officers

Vol 67

Place	Date	Hour	Summary of Events and Information	Remarks and references to Appendices
N.18d 7.3.	1-7-16 to 31-7-16		All batteries in action on Divisional front from O.1d 6½.½ to T6B.6.1½.	
	15/7/16		X Battery ordered to join 5th Australian Division	
	19/7/16		9.45" Heavy T.M received	
	28/7/16		X Battery relieved A36 TM. Bty	
	29/7/16		Y Battery relieved by Z battery 2nd Canadian Division	
	30/7/16		Y " " Y36 TM. Bty	

J. C. Hands Capt RA
50th Divl T.M.O

T2134. Wt. W708—776. 500000. 4/15. Sir J. C. & S.

Army Form C. 2118.

WAR DIARY
or
INTELLIGENCE SUMMARY. of 50th Divisional Trench Mortar Batteries

(Erase heading not required.)

Instructions regarding War Diaries and Intelligence Summaries are contained in F. S. Regs., Part II. and the Staff Manual respectively. Title pages will be prepared in manuscript.

AUGUST 1916 — VOLUME :- 2. — Vol 4

Place	Date	Hour	Summary of Events and Information	Remarks and references to Appendices
Sheet 28. M.18.a.8.0.	1/8/16		X. Y. & Z. Batteries 2" in action on Divisional Front.	
— " —	2/8/16		do	
— " —	3/8/16		do V Battery proceeded into action (9.45") on Divisional Front.	
— " —	4/8/16		X. Y & Z. Batteries 2" in action on Divisional Front. V. Battery preparing 9.45" for action.	
— " —	5/8/16		X. Y. & Z. Batteries in action on Divisional Front. V. Battery fired 25 rounds from Divl Front.	
— " —	6/8/16		X. Y. & Z. Batteries relieved personnel in trenches. V. Battery personnel returned to billets.	
— " —	7/8/16		X. Y. & Z. Batteries in action on Divisional Front.	
— " —	8/8/16		D.T.M. Officer 19th Division reported and inspected all T.M. positions on Divisional Front. X. Y. & Z. Btes in action on Divisional Front.	
— " — Sheet 27. Q.20.a.1.[illegible]	9/8/16		Relieved by 19th Division. Handed over all guns, (including one 9.45"), stores, ammunition etc; Personnel proceeded by march route to V Corps Rest Area (BUSSUS?)	
— " —	10/8/16		Training and instructional parades. Received 12 guns, 2" stores, from 19th Division	
— " —	11/8/16		do .	
Bois Bergues	12/8/16.		Personnel with guns, stores, etc; entrained to join RESERVE ARMY in the BERNAVILLE. AREA. Arrived at billets in this area about midnight.	

T2131. Wt. W708—776. 500000. 4/15. Sir J. C. & S.

On His Majesty's Service.

Army Form C. 2118.

Instructions regarding War Diaries and Intelligence Summaries are contained in F. S. Regs., Part II. and the Staff Manual respectively. Title Pages will be prepared in manuscript.

WAR DIARY
or
INTELLIGENCE SUMMARY of 50th Divisional Trench Mortar Batteries

(Erase heading not required.)

December 1917 Volume No. 18

Vol 24

Place	Date	Hour	Summary of Events and Information	Remarks and references to Appendices
Sheet 28				
B.15.a.2.4	1/12/17		Fatigues. Salving gun etc.	
– do –	2/12/17		– do –	
– do –	3/12/17		– do –	
– do –	4/12/17		– do –	
– do –	5/12/17		– do –	
– do –	6/12/17		– do –	
– do –	7/12/17		– do –	
– do –	8/12/17		– do –	
– do –	9/12/17		– do –	
– do –	10/12/17		– do – Medium and Heavy Batteries vacated camp at B.15.a.2.4 (Sheet 28) and proceeded to G.15.a. Sheet 28)	
G.15.a	11/12/17		Fatigues. Cleaning camp etc.	
– do –	12/12/17		Fatigues, Medium and Heavy Batteries vacated camp at G.15.a and proceeded to G.10.c.1.4.	
G.10.c.1.4.	13/12/17		Fatigues. Erecting Huts and general repairs to camp.	
– do –	14/12/17		Fatigues. Erecting Huts and general repairs to camp. Y50 Battery returned from Fifth Army T.M. School.	
– do –	15/12/17		Fatigues	
– do –	16/12/17		Fatigues. X50 Battery proceeded to Second Army T.M. School for course of instruction in T.M.	
– do –	17/12/17		Fatigues. Rifle Drill, Physical Drill, Foot Drill, Guard Mounting	
– do –	18/12/17		Full Marching Order, Inspection, Inspection of Box Respirators, Box Respirator Drill, Rifle Drill.	

2449 Wt. W14957/M90 750,000 1/16 J.B.C. & A. Forms/C.2118/12.

Army Form C. 2118.

WAR DIARY
or
INTELLIGENCE SUMMARY
(Erase heading not required.)

Instructions regarding War Diaries and Intelligence Summaries are contained in F. S. Regs., Part II. and the Staff Manual respectively. Title Pages will be prepared in manuscript.

Place	Date	Hour	Summary of Events and Information	Remarks and references to Appendices
G. 10. C. 14	19/12/17		Rifle Drill, Marching Drill Fatigues.	
– do –	20/12/17		Route March.	
– do –	21/12/17		Fatigues. V50 Battery proceeded to camp at I. 8. d. 1. 8. H. Qrs and Medium Batteries proceeded to G. 1. b. 4. 8	
G. 1. b. 4. 8	22/12/17		Fatigues, Salving Guns.	
– do –	23/12/17		— do —	
– do –	24/12/17		— do —	
– do –	25/12/17		— do —	
– do –	26/12/17		— do —	
– do –	27/12/17		— do —	
– do –	28/12/17		— do — H. Qrs, and Medium Batteries proceeded to I. 8. d. 1. 8.	
I. 8. d. 1. 8	29/12/17		Fatigues. Salving Guns.	
– do –	30/12/17		— do —	
– do –	31/12/17		— do —	

R. Macdonald Captain
o/50th D. T.M.O.

2449 Wt. W14957/M90 750,000 1/16 J.B.C. & A. Forms/C.2118/12.

WAR DIARY
or
INTELLIGENCE SUMMARY of 50th Divisional Trench Mortar Batteries.

Army Form C. 2118.

Instructions regarding War Diaries and Intelligence Summaries are contained in F. S. Regs., Part II. and the Staff Manual respectively. Title Pages will be prepared in manuscript.

(*Erase heading not required.*)

JANUARY 1918 VOLUME No: 19

Place	Date	Hour	Summary of Events and Information	Remarks and references to Appendices
E.3.d.1.8.	1/1/18		Fatigues. Salving guns etc:	
– do –	2/1/18.		— do. —	
– do –	3/1/18		— do —	
– do –	4/1/18		— do —	
– do –	5/1/18		— do — X.50 Battery rejoined from Second Army T. M. School.	
– do –	6/1/18		— do —	
– do –	7/1/18		— do — Headquarters, Y and Z/50 Battery's proceeded to new billets at G.7.b.4.8. X and Y.50 Battery's remaining in Forward Area.	
G.7.b.4.8.	8/1/18.		Fatigues. Salving guns etc: Rifle inspection.	
– do –	9/1/18		Route March. Fatigues.	
– do –	10/1/18.		— . do — .	
– do –	11/1/18		Squad Drill. Kit Inspection. X and Y/50 Battery's rejoined from Forward Area.	
– do –	12/1/18		Rifle and revolver Inspection. Fatigues.	
– do –	13/1/18		H.Qrs, Medium and Heavy Batteries vacated billets at G.7.b.4.8. and proceeded to billets at HARDIFORT. Fatigues.	
HARDIFORT.	14/1/18		H.Qrs, Medium and Heavy Batteries vacated billets at HARDIFORT and proceeded to billets at RENESCURE. Fatigues.	
RENESCURE	15/1/18		H.Qrs. Medium and Heavy Batteries vacated billets at RENESCURE and proceeded to billets at OLVE WERQUIN. Fatigues.	

2449 Wt. W14957/M90 750,000 1/16 J.B.C. & A. Forms/C.2118/12.

Army Form C. 2118.

Instructions regarding War Diaries and Intelligence Summaries are contained in F. S. Regs., Part II. and the Staff Manual respectively. Title Pages will be prepared in manuscript.

WAR DIARY
or
INTELLIGENCE SUMMARY
(Erase heading not required.)

Place	Date	Hour	Summary of Events and Information	Remarks and references to Appendices
OUVE WIRQUIN	16/1/18		Fatigues.	
— do —	17/1/18		Rifle, revolver, kit, box respirator and Iron ration inspection. Physical drill. Squad Drill.	
— do	18/1/18		Full marching order parade. route march. Rifle drill. Squad Drill. Lecture. "Care of box respirator" by D.A.G.O.	
— do —	19/1/18		Rifle drill. Physical drill. Box respirator drill. Squad drill.	
— do —	20/1/18		Lecture. Church Parade.	
— do —	21/1/18		Rifle drill and Guard mounting. Physical Drill. Squad drill. Full marching order parade.	
— do —	22/1/18		Full marching order inspection by D.T.M.O. Physical drill. Guard mounting. Rifle practice.	
— do —	23/1/18		Route March (Skeleton order) Lecture "Telephones".	
— do —	24/1/18		Rifle Drill. Physical drill Squad drill. Rifle practice (V/50 Battery) Fatigues. N.C.O's Lecture on Map reading.	
— do —	25/1/18		Physical drill, Bath parade. Box respirator drill. Telephony.	
— do —	26/1/18		Physical drill. Fatigues	
— do —	27/1/18		H.Qrs. Medium & Heavy Batteries vacated billets at OUVE WIRQUIN and proceeded by march route to RENESCURE. Fatigues.	
RENESCURE	28/1/18.		H.Qrs. Medium & Heavy Batteries vacated billets at RENESCURE and proceeded by march route to billets at HARDIFORT. Fatigues.	
HARDIFORT	29/1/18.		H.Qrs, Medium & Heavy Batteries vacated billets at HARDIFORT and proceeded by march route to billets at POPERINGHE.	
POPERINGHE.	30/1/18.		H.Qrs. Medium & Heavy Batteries vacated billets at POPERINGHE and proceeded by march route to billets at I.4.a.6.8. Rear billet at H.16.a.7.1.	
I.4.a.6.8.	31/1/18.		Fatigues.	

Mark S. [illegible] Captain
50th D.T.M.O.

2449 Wt. W14957/M90 750,000 1/16 J.B.C. & A. Forms/C.2118/12.

Instructions regarding War Diaries and Intelligence Summaries are contained in F. S. Regs., Part II. and the Staff Manual respectively. Title Pages will be prepared in manuscript.

WAR DIARY
or
INTELLIGENCE SUMMARY

of 50th DIVISIONAL TRENCH MORTAR BATTERIES

(Erase heading not required.)

Army Form C. 2118.

FEBRUARY 1918.

VOLUME No. XX

Vol 26

Place	Date	Hour	Summary of Events and Information	Remarks and references to Appendices
I.4.a.6.8.	1/2/18		Fatigues.	
— do —	2/2/18		Fatigues. Z/50 Battery proceeded to IV Army T.M. School on course of instruction.	
— do —	3/2/18		Fatigues, assisting R.E.s with O.P.s at PASSCHENDAELE etc.	
— do —	4/2/18		Fatigues. do	
— do —	5/2/18		Fatigues. do	
— do —	6/2/18		Fatigues. do	
— do —	7/2/18		Fatigues. do	
— do —	8/2/18		Fatigues. do	
— do —	9/2/18		Fatigues. do	
— do —	10/2/18		Fatigues. do	
— do —	11/2/18		Fatigues. Party of X/50 and Y/50 Battery's preparing emplacements for 6" Mortars at D.17.c.5.7.	
— do —	12/2/18		Fatigues. do	
— do —	13/2/18		Fatigues. do	
— do —	14/2/18		Fatigues. do	
— do —	15/2/18		Fatigues. do	
— do —	16/2/18		Fatigues. do	
— do —	17/2/18		Fatigues. do	
— do —	18/2/18		Fatigues. do	
— do —	19/2/18		Fatigues. do	
— do —	20/2/18		Fatigues. do	
— do —	21/2/18		Fatigues. do	
— do —	22/2/18		Fatigues. Batteries relieved by personnel of 33rd Divisional T.M. Btys. Billets at I.4.a.6.8. vacated and proceeded to billets at HARDIFORT, by lorry	
HARDIFORT	23/2/18		Vacated billets at HARDIFORT and proceeded to billets at OUVE WIRQUIN	
OUVE WIRQUIN	24/2/18		Inspection of kit, rifles, revolvers, box respirators etc.	
— do —	25/2/18		Route march, Squad, Physical, Rifle drill. Z/50 Battery rejoined from III Army T.M. School.	
— do —	26/2/18		— do —	
— do —	27/2/18		Route march, Rifle drill, Recreational training	
— do —	28/2/18		Physical, Box respirator, Squad drill, [illegible], Lecture on telephone	

[illegible] Captain R.A.
50th D.T.M.B.

2449 Wt. W14957/M90 750,000 1/16 J.B.C. & A. Forms/C.2118/12.

50th (Northumbrian) Artillery.

50th DIVISIONAL TRENCH MORTARS

MARCH 1918

Instructions regarding War Diaries and Intelligence Summaries are contained in F. S. Regs., Part II. and the Staff Manual respectively. Title Pages will be prepared in manuscript.

WAR DIARY
or
INTELLIGENCE SUMMARY of 50th Divisional Trench Mortar Batteries

(*Erase heading not required.*)

Army Form C. 2118.

March 1918. Volume No. 21

Place	Date	Hour	Summary of Events and Information	Remarks and references to Appendices
[illegible] WIRQUIN	1/3/18		Physical, Semaphore, Morse & Rifle Drill. Lecture: Economy of Government Stores.	
— do —	2/3/18		Physical & Squad Drill. Telephony. Lecture "Musketry".	
— do —	3/3/18		Church Parade.	
— do —	4/3/18		Route March. Rifle practice.	
— do —	5/3/18		Physical Drill. Telephone Class. Gun Drill & Laying. Rifle Practice.	
— do —	6/3/18		Physical Drill. Gun Drill and Laying. Telephone Class. Rifle Drill. Lecture. Rifle Practice.	
— do —	7/3/18		Physical Drill. Instruction in Bombing. Gun Drill. Telephony.	
— do —	8/3/18		Route March. Lecture by D.R.C.O. Instruction in Bombing.	
THENNES	9/3/18		X & Y.50 Batteries proceeded by train from St OMER to MOREUIL. HQrs proceeded by road arriving at THENNES about 6.0 pm.	
— do —	10/3/18		X & Y.50 Batteries arrived at billets at THENNES. Fatigues.	
— do —	11/3/18		Fatigues.	
— do —	12/3/18		HQrs, X & Y.50 Batteries proceeded by road to billets at CHUIGNOLLES, arriving about 7.45 pm. Fatigues	
CHUIGNOLLES	13/3/18		Fatigues. Gun Drill. Route March.	
— do —	14/3/18		Fatigues. Gun Drill.	
— do —	15/3/18		Fatigues. HQrs X & Y.50 Batteries proceeded by road to billets at BUIRE arriving about 3.40 pm.	
BUIRE	16/3/18		Inspection. Kit. Marching Order. Fatigues. Cleaning Guns etc.	
— do —	17/3/18		Fatigues	
· do ·	18/3/18		· do ·	
· do ·	19/3/18		· do ·	
· do ·	20/3/18		· do ·	
· do ·	21/3/18		· do ·	
· do ·	22/3/18		Vacated billets at BUIRE and proceeded to billets at FAUCAUCOURT	
FAUCAUCOURT	23/3/18		— — — FAUCAUCOURT — — — — CHUIGNOLLES	
CHUIGNOLLES	24/3/18		Fatigues	
· do ·	25/3/18		Vacated billets at CHUIGNOLLES and proceeded to billets at HAMEL	

2449 Wt. W14957/M90 750,000 1/16 J.B.C. & A. Forms/C.2118/12.

Army Form C. 2118.

WAR DIARY
or
INTELLIGENCE SUMMARY
(Erase heading not required.)

Instructions regarding War Diaries and Intelligence Summaries are contained in F. S. Regs., Part II. and the Staff Manual respectively. Title Pages will be prepared in manuscript.

Place	Date	Hour	Summary of Events and Information	Remarks and references to Appendices
HAMEL	26/3/18		Vacated billets at HAMEL and proceeded to billets at MARCEL-CAVE, 40 other ranks attached to D.A.C.	
MARCEL CAVE	27/3/18		— — — MARCEL CAVE & — — — BOVES 20 other ranks attached D.A.C. & 3 officers	
BOVES	28/3/18		— — — BOVES and — — — SOURDON 16 other ranks attached D.A.C. & 4 officers.	
SOURDON	29/3/18		— — — SOURDON — — — BOVES.	
BOVES.	30/3/18		Fatigues	
— do —	31/3/18.		— do. —	

N. C[illegible]
Captain R.A.
50th D. T. M. O.

2449 Wt. W14957/M90 750,000 1/16 J.B.C. & A. Forms/C.2118/12.

50TH DIVISIONAL TRENCH MORTAR BATTERIES APRIL 1918

Army Form C. 2118.

WAR DIARY
or
INTELLIGENCE SUMMARY OF 50TH DIVISIONAL TRENCH MORTAR BATTERIES
(Erase heading not required.)

Instructions regarding War Diaries and Intelligence Summaries are contained in F. S. Regs., Part II. and the Staff Manual respectively. Title Pages will be prepared in manuscript.

APRIL 1918

VOLUME Nº 22

Vol 28

Place	Date	Hour	Summary of Events and Information	Remarks and references to Appendices
BOVES	1.4.18		Fatigues	
-do-	2.4.18		-do-	
-do-	3.4.18		-do-	
-do-	4.4.18		Vacated billets at BOVES and proceeded to billets at SAINS-LES-AMIENOIS.	
SAINS-LES-AMIENOIS	5.4.18		Fatigues	
-do-	6.4.18		-do-	
-do-	7.4.18		-do-	
-do-	8.4.18		-do-	
-do-	9.4.18		Vacated billets at SAINS-LES-AMIENOIS and proceeded to billets at DU-PONT-DE-METZ.	
DU-PONT-DE-METZ	10.4.18		Vacated billets at DU-PONT-DE-METZ and proceeded to billets at DOMQUEUR.	
DOMQUEUR	11.4.18		Vacated billets at DOMQUEUR and proceeded to billets at BLANGERVAL.	
BLANGERVAL	12.4.18		Vacated billets at BLANGERVAL and proceeded to billets at TANGRY.	
TANGRY	13.4.18		Vacated billets at TANGRY and proceeded to billets at ST. HILAIRE	
ST. HILAIRE	14.4.18		Vacated billets at St. HILAIRE and proceeded to billets at LAPUGNOY.	
LAPUGNOY	15.4.18		Vacated billets at LAPUGNOY and proceeded to billets at OBLINGHEM, on relief of 3rd T.Ms. in action, and took over 3. 6" Newton T.M.s covering 4th Div: Front.	
OBLINGHEM	16.4.18	36A.	Fatigues, X and Y 50 Batteries in action preparing positions and ammunition dumps	
-do-	17.4.18		Fatigues, X and Y 50 Batteries in action. Received 4 6" T.Ms from Ordnance.	
-do-	18.4.18		X & Y. 50 Batteries in action. 72 rounds fired during attack, by the enemy.	
-do-	19.4.18		X & Y. 50 Batteries in action 68 rounds fired during the day, on M.G. Posts etc.	
-do-	20.4.18		X & Y. 50 Batteries in action. 15 rounds fired into PACAUT WOOD. 38 rounds into HOUSE and PONTOON Q 33.c.2.6. Several direct hits obtained. 45 rounds fired on M.G. Posts in front edge of ORCHARD. W.11 a. 9.5. for registration and effect. Received 2. 9.45" T.Ms.	
-do-	21.4.18		X & Y 50 Batteries in action. 37 rounds fired on W.4c.45.75 & M.G's in ORCHARD. W.11a and b. 9.45" registered on HOUSE. Q.33.a.95.45.	
-do-	22.4.18		X & Y 50 Batteries in action. 43 rounds 9.45" and 129 rounds 6" fired during offensive operations between 5.15 - 5.45 am	
-do-	23.4.18		X & Y.50 Batteries in action. cleaning & general improvement to positions and guns. Vacated billets at OBLINGHEM at 3.15 pm owing to hostile shelling and proceeded to billets at CHOCQUES.	
-do-	24/4/18		X & Y.50 Batteries in action preparing guns and checking ammunition ready for handing over. Handed over guns in line and billets and all ammunition to 4th Divisional Trench Mortars & took over 9 mortars from 4th Division at CHOCQUES.	
-do-	25/4/18		Fatigues. Vacated billets at CHOCQUES, and proceeded to billets at NEDON.	
NEDON	26/4/18		Fatigues. Inspection of kit, Equipment, Box Respirators, etc.	
-do-	27/4/18		Rifle Drill. Foot Drill. Fatigues.	
-do-	28/4/18		Route March. Squad Drill. Physical Drill. Fatigues.	
-do-	29/4/18		Rifle Drill. Squad Drill. Fatigues.	
-do-	30/4/18		HQs & Batteries vacated billets at NEDON at 8.0 AM & proceeded to LAPUGNOY to entrain for SOISSONS Area. Left LAPUGNOY en-route at 1.30 pm	D. C. Hauck Capt R.A. 50th D.T.M.O.

2449 Wt. W14957/M90 750,000 1/16 J.B.C. & A. Forms/C.2118/12.

WAR DIARY
or
INTELLIGENCE SUMMARY.
(Erase heading not required.)

Army Form C. 2118.

Instructions regarding War Diaries and Intelligence Summaries are contained in F. S. Regs., Part II. and the Staff Manual respectively. Title pages will be prepared in manuscript.

50th T.M. Batteries

Vol 29

Place	Date	Hour	Summary of Events and Information	Remarks and references to Appendices
M & D	Aug			
[illegible]	1st	[illegible]	Arrived Crugny	
No. 2.1	2nd		T.M. Batteries rest. Parades. Gun Drill, Squad Drill, Rifle Drill	
	3rd		Gun Drill. Telephone Class, Rifle Drill Squad Drill	
	4th		" " " " "	
	5th		Moved from Crugny to [illegible]	
	6th–10th		do. [illegible]	
	11th		Moved [illegible] to [illegible] – P.C. Calvaire	
	[illegible]		X Battery worked on positions in Tranch D'Orleans and positions on Craonne Plateau. Y battery worked on positions in Tranch D'Orleans and Bois de Butte[s].	
	[illegible]		Work continued on all T.M. Positions.	
	19th		X battery H.Q. moved to Craonne plateau. Some new positions [illegible]. Y Battery moved all guns from Tranche D'ORLEANS to Craonne plateau. Work commenced on [illegible] positions. X Battery fired 12 rounds to register 4 guns.	

1577 Wt. W10791/1773 500,000 1/15 D. D. & L. A.D.S.S./Forms/C. 2118.

Army Form C. 2118.

Instructions regarding War Diaries and Intelligence Summaries are contained in F. S. Regs., Part II. and the Staff Manual respectively. Title pages will be prepared in manuscript.

WAR DIARY ~~or~~ ~~INTELLIGENCE SUMMARY.~~ 50th T.M. Batteries.

(Erase heading not required.)

Place	Date	Hour	Summary of Events and Information	Remarks and references to Appendices
MAP Berry-au-Bac			Work continued on all positions on plateau.	
No. 0.	20th		X complete work on four positions.	
	21st		Work continued on positions. Ammunition being carried to guns.	
	22nd 23rd		Work continued.	
	24th		Y battery fired 6 rounds in registration	
			X battery " 4 " in registration.	
	25th		Work completed on 4 positions of X Battery. Ammunition being carried to all guns.	
	26th		Works continued. All guns registered.	
	27th	1 AM	Enemy barrage put down. S.O.S fired.	
		4.30 AM	Enemy attack commenced. All T.M.s fired on S.O.S lines and continued firing until enemy were on positions. Guns were blown up and detachment attempted to retire. 5 Officers and 81 O.R missing.	
			R. Macleod Capt D.T.M.O.	15.6.18

1577 Wt. W10791/1773 500,000 1/15 D. D. & L. A.D.S.S./Forms/C. 2118.

Instructions regarding War Diaries and Intelligence Summaries are contained in F. S. Regs., Part II. and the Staff Manual respectively. Title pages will be prepared in manuscript.

WAR DIARY ~~or~~ ~~INTELLIGENCE SUMMARY.~~ OF 50TH DIV. TRENCH MORTAR BTY'S

(Erase heading not required.)

Army Form C. 2118.

JUNE 1918 VOLUME XXXIX

Place	Date	Hour	Summary of Events and Information	Remarks and references to Appendices
COURJONNET.	1-6-18 to 3-6-18		ATTACHED TO S.A.A. SECTION 50TH D.A.C. FOR FATIGUES	
NEAR LAGNY	3-6-18		MOVED TO LES EPEES FARM.	
NEAR LAGNY.	3-6-18 to 23-6-18		ATTACHED TO S.A.A. SECTION 50TH D.A.C. FOR FATIGUES	
VERDEY.	24-6-18		MOVED TO VERDEY.	
	25-6-18		RECEIVED REINFORCEMENTS	
VERDEY	to 30-6-18		TRAINING OF REINFORCEMENTS	

FIELD 30-6-18.

R. Macleod CAPT.
50TH D.T.M.O.

D. D. & L., London, E.C. (A8093) Wt. W1171/M2031 750,000 5/17 Sch. 52 Forms C2118/14

Instructions regarding War Diaries and Intelligence Summaries are contained in F. S. Regs., Part II. and the Staff Manual respectively. Title pages will be prepared in manuscript.

WAR DIARY of 50TH DIV. TRENCH MORTAR. BATTERIES. or ~~INTELLIGENCE SUMMARY.~~

(Erase heading not required.)

Army Form C. 2118.

JULY 1918.

Vol 31

Place	Date	Hour	Summary of Events and Information	Remarks and references to Appendices
VERDEY. (MARNE)	1-7-18 TO 2-7-18		TRAINING OF BATTERIES	
-do-	3-7-18		MOVED TO FERE CHAMPENOISE (MARNE) AND ENTRAINED.	
	4-7-18		DETRAINED AT LONGPRE. AND MOVED TO BETTENCOURT-RIVIERE (SOMME)	
BETTENCOURT-RIVIERE (SOMME)	5-7-18 TO 27-7-18		TRAINING OF BATTERIES.	
-do-	28-7-18		MOVED TO CAMP AT ECCART FARM. (N.W. CORNER OF. BOIS DE LA CROIX DE PIERRE.)	
ECCART FARM.	29-7-18 TO 31-7-18		TRAINING OF BATTERIES.	

R Macleod CAPT.
50TH D.T.M.O.
FIELD 31-7-18.

D. D. & L., London, E.C. (A8001) Wt. W1771/M2031 750,000 5/17 Sch. 52 Forms C2118/14

Instructions regarding War Diaries and Intelligence Summaries are contained in F. S. Regs., Part II. and the Staff Manual respectively. Title pages will be prepared in manuscript.

WAR DIARY of 50TH DIV. TRENCH MORTAR BATTERIES. or INTELLIGENCE SUMMARY.

Army Form C. 2118.

(Erase heading not required.)

Place	Date	Hour	Summary of Events and Information	Remarks and references to Appendices
VERDEY (MARNE)	1-4-18 to 2-4-18		TRAINING OF BATTERIES.	
– do –	3-4-18		MOVED TO FERE CHAMPENOISE (MARNE) AND ENTRAINED.	
	4-4-18		DETRAINED AT LONGPRE AND MOVED TO BETTENCOURT-RIVIERE (SOMME)	
BETTENCOURT-RIVIERE (SOMME)	5-4-18 to 27-4-18		TRAINING OF BATTERIES.	
– do –	28-4-18		MOVED TO CAMP AT ECCART FARM (N.W. CORNER OF BOIS DE LA CROIX DE PIERRE)	
ECCART FARM	29-4-18 to 31-4-18		TRAINING OF BATTERIES.	

R. Macleod
Capt
50th D.T.M.O.
FIELD 31-4-18

D. D. & L., London, E.C. (A7091) Wt. W1391/M1031 750,000 5/17 Sch 52 Forms C2118/14

Instructions regarding War Diaries and Intelligence Summaries are contained in F. S. Regs., Part II. and the Staff Manual respectively. Title pages will be prepared in manuscript.

WAR DIARY
or
~~INTELLIGENCE SUMMARY.~~
(Erase heading not required.)

50TH DIVISIONAL TRENCH MORTAR BATTERIES.
No. ....
Date August 1918

Army Form C. 2118.

Vol 32

VOL XLI

Place	Date	Hour	Summary of Events and Information	Remarks and references to Appendices
	1st		X/50 MOVED FROM CAMP AT ECCART FARM (N.W. CORNER BOIS DE LA CROIX DE PIERRE) TO HEILLY HQRS. J4b.1.4.	
	2nd		X/50 RELIEVED THE 9TH AUST. BTY. HQRS HEILLY J4b.1.4. Y/50 MOVED FROM CAMP AT ECCART FARM TO PONT NOYELLES AND ATTACHED TO 50TH DAC AND 58TH DAC FOR FATIGUES ON AMMUNITION DUMPS.	
	4th		X/50 AT J30b 90.25 FIRED 4 RDS REGISTRATION ON SAILLY LAURETTE.	
	6th		HOSTILE RAID DURING EARLY MORNING. 1 NCO AND 1 GUNNER MISSING FROM GUN POSITION AT J30c 65.35	
	7th		X/50 FIRED 20 RDS ON SAILLY LAURETTE. Y/50 MOVED FROM PONT NOYELLES TO HQRS. HEILLY.	
	8th		DURING EARLY MORNING ATTACK ON ENEMY POSITIONS X/50 AT J30b. 90.25. FIRED 60 RDS ON SAILLY LAURETTE. (1 GUNNER SLIGHTLY WOUNDED).	
	9th to 11th		PERSONNELL OF BOTH BATTERIES ENGAGED IN REMOVAL OF GUNS AND AMMUNITION.	
	12th		MOVED TO VAUX. HQRS AT. [illegible]21d 2.3	
	13th to 15th		PERSONNEL OF BOTH BATTERIES ENGAGED IN SALVAGE OF GUNS AND AMMUNITION.	
	16th to 20th		2 OFFICERS AND 40 OTHER RANKS DETACHED ON FATIGUES FOR 250 BDE. HQRS. REMAINDER ON SALVAGE WORK.	
	21st to 23rd		PARTY AT 250 BDE HQRS REJOINED. BATTERIES ON SALVAGE WORK.	
	24th to 28th		X/50 PROCEEDED TO SAILLY FLIBEAUCOURT FOR T.M COURSE AT 4TH ARMY. SCHOOL. Y/50 ENGAGED ON FATIGUES AND SALVAGE WORK.	
	29th to 31st		Y/50 MOVED TO BRAY. HQRS L15d 4.2. FATIGUES.	

	HEAVY TRENCH MORTARS.	MEDIUM TRENCH MORTARS	LIGHT TRENCH MORTARS
HOSTILE TRENCH MORTARS SALVAGED DURING MONTH.	2.	4.	14.
— do — AMMUNITION.	GRANATENWERFER. 350 RDS.		LIGHT MINENWERFER 280 RDS

R. Muchard[?] CAPT.
50TH DTMO

D. D. & L., London, E.C.
(A10266) Wt W5300/P713 750,000 2/18 Sch. 52 Forms/C2118/16

Instructions regarding War Diaries and Intelligence Summaries are contained in F. S. Regs., Part II. and the Staff Manual respectively. Title pages will be prepared in manuscript.

WAR DIARY
or
INTELLIGENCE SUMMARY.
(Erase heading not required.)

Army Form C. 2118.

Vol 33

Place	Date	Hour	Summary of Events and Information	Remarks and references to Appendices
			X/50 ON TRENCH MORTAR COURSE AT THE 4TH ARMY ARTILLERY SCHOOL.	
	1ST		Y/50 MOVED FROM BRAY. (SOMME) TO PAS. (PAS DE CALAIS)	
	2ND		Y/50 MOVED FROM PAS TO ARRAS. HEADQUARTERS RUE BLANC PIGNON ARRAS.	
	3RD TO 8TH		Y/50 ENGAGED IN MAKING GUN PITS IN THE LINE AT J32c.5.1. SHEET. 51B	
	9TH		Y/50. TWO 6" TRENCH MORTARS IN ACTION. FIRED 20 RDS ON ENEMY WIRE AT J26d.6.5.	
	10TH		Y/50. FIRED 40 RDS ON ENEMY WIRE AT J32d 6.5 TO J32d.6.45. 1 MAN WOUNDED (GAS). RELEIVED IN THE LINE AT 7.0PM BY THE 11TH DIV. T.M. BTYS.	
	11TH		Y/50 MOVED FROM ARRAS TO CAMP AT MAROEUIL. F24B 9.2. SHEET 51C.	
	12TH		Y/50 FATIGUES.	
	13TH		Y/50 MOVED FROM CAMP TO BILLETS IN MAROEUIL.	
	14TH		Y/50 FATIGUES	
	15TH		Y/50 FATIGUES. X/50 REJOINED FROM 4TH ARMY ARTILLERY SCHOOL.	
	16TH TO 18TH		FATIGUES AND TRAINING (GUN DRILL. RIFLE DRILL. MARCHING DRILL. GUN-PIT DIGGING)	
	19TH TO 22ND		X/50 ATTACHED 50TH DAC ON SALVAGE OF AMMUNITION. Y/50 ON FATIGUES AND TRAINING (RIFLE DRILL. MARCHING DRILL. GUN DRILL AND LAYING.)	
	23RD		X/50 REJOINED. FATIGUES.	
	24TH TO 28TH		TRAINING (GUN DRILL + LAYING. RIFLE DRILL. MARCHING DRILL. TELEPHONISTS CLASSES. N.C.O'S CLASS (MAP READING) AND REVOLVER PRACTISE. (FULL MARCHING ORDER INSPECTION AND ROUTE MARCH.)	
	29TH		Y/50. PROCEED ON A TRENCH MORTAR COURSE AT THE 4TH ARMY SCHOOL OF MORTARS.	
	29TH TO 30TH		X/50 TRAINING AND FATIGUES.	

R. Macleod CAPT
50TH D.T.M.O.

D. D. & L., London, E.C.
(A10266) Wt W5300/P713 750,000 2/18 Sch. 52 Forms/C2118/16

Army Form C. 2118.

Instructions regarding War Diaries and Intelligence Summaries are contained in F. S. Regs., Part II. and the Staff Manual respectively. Title pages will be prepared in manuscript.

WAR DIARY of 50TH DIV. T.M. BTYS

or

~~INTELLIGENCE SUMMARY.~~ OCTOBER. 1918.

(Erase heading not required.)

VOLUME. XLIII

Vol 34

Place	Date	Hour	Summary of Events and Information	Remarks and references to Appendices
	1st to 13th		Y/50. T.M.B. ON COURSE AT THE 1ST ARMY SCHOOL OF MORTARS	
	1st to 6th		X/50 T.M.B. AT MAROEUIL. TRAINING (GUN DRILL. RIFLE DRILL. MARCHING DRILL. TELEPHONISTS CLASSES. NCOS MAP READING CLASSES.)	
	4th		X/50. T.M.B. RELIEVED 20TH DIV. T.M. BTYS. HQRS. S.24.A.80. LINE HQRS AT S.6.D.45.95. AND T.20.D.50.25. SHEET 44A.	
	5th to 11th		SALVAGING OF 6" T.M. AMMUNITION	
	12th		RELIEVED BY 12TH DIV. T.M. BTYS. AND MOVED TO AGNIERES	
	13th		Y/50 RETURNED TO AGNIERES FROM 1ST ARMY SCHOOL OF MORTARS.	
	14th		X/50 ENTRAINED AT AUBIGNY. Y/50 ENTRAINED AT ACQ.	
	15th		X/50 DETRAINED AT PERONNE. Y/50 DETRAINED AT TINCOURT (BATTERIES MOVED TO TEMPLEUX-LA-FOSSE.)	
	16th to 25th		TRAINING OF BATTERIES (GUN DRILL. RIFLE DRILL. MARCHING DRILL. NCOS REVOLVER PRACTISE AND MAP READING TELEPHONISTS CLASSES.).	
	26th		MOVED TO MARETZ.	
	27th to 30th		TRAINING OF BATTERIES (RIFLE DRILL. MARCHING DRILL. ROUTE MARCHING.)	
	31st.		MOVED TO LE CATEAU.	

W. Johnson
Capt
for 50th D.T.M.O.

D. D. & L., London, E.C.
(A10266) Wt W5300/P713 750,000 2/18 Sch. 52 Forms/C2118/16

Instructions regarding War Diaries and Intelligence Summaries are contained in F. S. Regs., Part II. and the Staff Manual respectively. Title pages will be prepared in manuscript.

WAR DIARY or INTELLIGENCE SUMMARY.

(Erase heading not required.)

OF 50TH DIV TRENCH MORTAR BATTERIES NOVEMBER. 1918.

Army Form C. 2118.

35

Place	Date	Hour	Summary of Events and Information	Remarks and references to Appendices
	1ST.		MONTAY.	
	2ND		MOVED TO BOUSIES.	
	3RD		MOVED TO FONTAINE-AU-BOIS	
	4TH TO 7TH		RECONNAISSANCE OF ROUTES. REPAIRING OF ROADS MAKING TRACKS BRIDGE BUILDING FOR 50TH D.A. BETWEEN FONTAINE-AU-BOIS, SASSEGNIES AND NOYELLES.	
	8TH TO 10TH		REPAIRING ROADS. MAKING TRACKS AND BRIDGE BUILDING FOR 50TH D.A IN THE NEIGHBOURHOOD OF SASSEGNIES AND NOYELLES.	
	10TH TO 18.		MOVED TO ST. REMY CHAUSSEE. TRAINING. PHYSICAL TRAINING, RIFLE DRILL, MARCHING DRILL, GUARD MOUNTING, ROUTE MARCHING. (INSPECTIONS FULL MARCHING ORDER AND KIT.)	
	19TH TO 30TH		MOVED TO DIMONT. SALVAGE WORK.	

R. S. Rackard[?] CAPT 50TH D.T.M.O.

D. D. & L., London, E.C. (A10266) Wt W5300/P713 750,000 2/16 Sch. 52 Forms/C2118/16

50TH DIVISIONAL TRENCH MORTAR BATTERIES

Army Form C. 2118.

WAR DIARY
or
INTELLIGENCE SUMMARY.
(*Erase heading not required.*) VOLUME XLV

Instructions regarding War Diaries and Intelligence Summaries are contained in F. S. Regs., Part II. and the Staff Manual respectively. Title pages will be prepared in manuscript.

Place	Date	Hour	Summary of Events and Information DECEMBER 1918	Remarks and references to Appendices
	1ST TO 5TH		AT DIMONT (NORD) SALVAGE AND EDUCATIONAL TRAINING	98/36
	6TH		MOVED TO SASSEGNIES	
	7TH TO 21ST		EDUCATIONAL TRAINING, PHYSICAL TRAINING	
	22ND		MOVED TO GOMMEGNIES	
	23RD TO 27TH		PHYSICAL TRAINING, EDUCATIONAL TRAINING	
	27TH		43 OFFICERS AND OTHER RANKS ATTACHED TO 50TH D.A.C	
	28TH TO 31ST		PHYSICAL TRAINING AND FATIGUES	

R. Machon CAPTAIN
50TH D.T.M.O

D. D. & L., London, E.C.
(…66) Wt W5300/P713 750,000 2/18 Sch. 52 Forms/C2118/16

50TH DIVISIONAL TRENCH MORTAR BATTERIES

Army Form C. 2118.

WAR DIARY
or
INTELLIGENCE SUMMARY.
(Erase heading not required.)

Instructions regarding War Diaries and Intelligence Summaries are contained in F. S. Regs., Part II. and the Staff Manual respectively. Title pages will be prepared in manuscript.

VOLUME XLVI

WO 37

Place	Date	Hour	Summary of Events and Information	Remarks and references to Appendices
			JANUARY 1919	
GOMMEGNIES	1st TO 31st		Physical training and fatigues.	

R. Rudd[illegible] CAPTAIN 50TH D.T.M.O.

D. D. & L., London, E.C.
(A10266) Wt W5300/P713 750,000 2/18 Sch. 52 Forms/C2118/16

www.ingramcontent.com/pod-product-compliance
Lightning Source LLC
Chambersburg PA
CBHW082012220426
43670CB00014B/2610
* 9 7 8 1 4 7 4 5 2 7 7 4 3 *